Encouraging Stories in the Bible

Dr. Daniel Kazemian

NEW HARBOR PRESS

Rapid City, SD

Kazemian/New Harbor Press
1601 Mt. Rushmore Rd, Ste 3288
Rapid City, SD 57701
www.NewHarborPress.com

Ordering Information:
Quantity sales. Special discounts are available on quantity pur-
chases by corporations, associations, and others. For details,
contact the "Special Sales Department" at the address above.

Encouraging Stories in the Bible/Dr. Daniel Kazemian-2nd ed.
ISBN 978-1-63357-186-0

Contents

About This Book

IT IS A PRIVILEGE to write this book by the direction of the Lord Jesus to encourage you to become knowledgeable in all stories in the Bible. This book will reach many Christian believers around the world.

My purpose is to summarize the stories in the Bible that could be better understood. I am able to share many beautiful stories about God's wonders from His Word with you and make them come alive to you.

I have used all marvelous stories with short stories to support you and build up your Christian life. I have tried to present my experience, which I have stored up in many years of my Christian walk with the Lord.

So, you may receive power and courage from the Lord. I believe the Lord Jesus has anointed this book. You may study it for your personal journey with the Lord to make you a better servant of God.

Many churches around the world will receive greater knowledge out of this book. I believe it will make them ready to share these wonderful stories with others.

This is a dynamic book that will allow you to become more informed and to mak a change in your personal life. This book will carry the presence of the Lord anytime you read it and hold it in your hand.

You will have a sense of anointing of the Lord that will be released in your life. I've prayed and spent time in God's presence in order to write this book. I know that God will meet you where you are. He is there to teach you and fill you with His Word.

Whenever you read this book, He will reach you and reveal Himself to you. He will change your life into a victorious Christian life, both for you and for your family. Blessed be in the name of the Lord Jesus. Amen.

Encouragement Words:

Encouragement is my favorite act of serving. I cherish giving the word and receiving a word from the wise person in the right place. It is extremely significant to build each other up with a word of faith and love.

I am reminded of this verse;

"Pleasant words *are like* a honeycomb, Sweetness to the soul, and health to the bones." Proverbs 16:24, NKJV.

I love the remark: **"pleasant words."** I like a word with positive expression and an exciting message to build up our faith.

We will strengthen each other with the knowledge of Words. Declare to ourselves how much the Lord Jesus loves us, and He cares for us all.

This verse also says that as **"a honeycomb,"** a sweet word gives us a taste of excitement. The Lord is offering to demonstrate how wonderful is His love for us and how He has never forsaken us.

The next phrase refers to **"health to the bones."** It means that a word of encouragement is extremely important for us to hear over and over again.

It will inspire and help us to get healing in our bodies and to have healthy bones. A word can strengthen our bones and release a healthy life for us.

We truly desire to get the Word and listening to a word of encouragement from someone whom God has chosen.

In this book, we will be looking at many verses and stories from the Bible. Then, how can we learn by opening our hearts and getting inspired by the Word?

We will be learning and growing in the spirit and building up a good foundation of our faith. Hearing the Word and serving other Christian believers. We will be reading many stories from the Old Testament and the New Testament.

As, we review all-powerful stories with brief records in the Bible. I believe every part of the Word of God; every story can teach us and lead us into our destiny.

The Story of Noah

THE STORY OF NOAH is very familiar to everyone who has heard it numerous times in many places. We have learned from Sunday school to the Bible study group.

God formed the earth and all the inhabitants in seven days. He created Adam and Eve, whom He told to multiply throughout the earth. God has seen that the earth is not living according to His plan,

He ordered everything according to His Word with God's protection. God handed over the free choice to human beings to choose what to believe, what to decide for himself.

How to survive without God, whether to worship Him or not? It's free will, how to love, and how to hate.

Even though humans were not fully aware of how their sins would lead to darkness and destruction of their lives. As we know, after Adam and Eve fell into sin, the wickedness of sin appeared to increase in the world.

The plan of God was for human beings, pure and blameless. God wants them to live in peace and joy. The spirit of sin was set up to transfer from generation to generation because God has created humans in spirit and soul and body.

Noah had a Favor:

There was a man named Noah, and he was a farmer. He was a righteous man among the people of the earth.

He found favor in the sight of God. The Lord chose him to carry an enormous plan. He was very obedient to the direction of God.

"And Noah began to be a farmer, and he planted a vineyard." Genesis 9:20, NKJV.

The Lord knew that he would fulfill the assignment and do the plan of God. Noah had such an obedient to the task he was given.

He would build up an Ark; it was a huge project for him. But the word of God came to him to complete the plan of God. Noah was living with an honorable life and was pleasing in the sight of God.

The Lord recognized that Noah could do the work of the Ark, which would take years to finish. He could fulfill what God instructed him to do.

The Ark and Flood:

God directed Noah on what size and design the Ark it should build up. At the same time, God allowed all the other people to decide for themselves in 120 years to repent and follow Him.

But all the people turned Him down before the floodwaters came forth. After heavy rain, the flood wiped out all creatures, and nearly all the people perished who were on the earth.

Only eight people, members of Noah's family, survived the devastation of the flood. After the flood, everything was diminished; almost nothing was left. These few members of the human race started a fresh new life on the earth together.

God declared to Noah that all humankind would never be wiped out again through another flood. He presented him with the rainbow as the sign that He would keep His word throughout all the generations to come.

The Word said Noah was 600 years old already when the flood occurred. God gave Noah 350 more years to live after the flood, and he died at the age of 950.

"Noah was six hundred years old when the floodwaters were on the earth." Genesis 7:6, NKJV.

The Story of Abraham

THIS STORY OF FAITH involves a powerful word of encouragement for us. We can grow into stable believers in our daily walk with God.

Abraham took an incredible journey in his life, turning into a mighty ministry of faith. He came from the town of Ur, and God told him to move out from his home to Haran, which is north of Canaan.

He became so obedient to the call of God that he could hear every Word of God. He heard God's voice that spoke to Abraham, and he followed the plan of God. After that, he would be established in the land of Canaan.

After that, God would establish him in the land of Canaan. When God called him to a land where he didn't know, he became the first Jew. But he surrendered himself to the command of God.

Abraham left his Home:

The Lord told him to leave his home, including his father's house and his family. God was showing him an unknown land.

Later a new descendant would be established through him. Jewish nations would rise to become God's chosen people.

One of his descendants shall be the Savior of the nations and the people of the world. God chose him, and his people would become a great nation, which is now called Israel.

Abraham Descendants:

God promised Abraham a son who would be the heir of the covenant. God builds up a nation that would multiply over the face of the earth.

God established that one of those descendants would be a blessing to all the nations of the world. According to the Law, as it was said, Abraham was the first Jew; he was also called a Hebrew.

God established a covenant with Abraham and his descendants. He would become a father of nations; his descendants would be as numerous as the stars. The Lord will bless all the nations of the earth through Abraham, Isaac, and Jacob.

"Get out of your country,

From your family

And from your father's house,

To a land that I will show you.

I will make you a great nation;

I will bless you

And make your name great;

And you shall be a blessing.

I will bless those who bless you,

And I will curse him who curses you;

And in you all the families of the earth shall be blessed." Genesis 12:1-3, NKJV.

Promised a Son:

This is an encouraging word for us. We can take into our spirit as we meditate on the Word of God and His goodness. Abraham thought the promise of God would be impossible to get fulfilled.

Because he was 100 years and Sarah was 90 years old. He made a wrong decision to rush quickly into conceiving a son with Hagar, who was not chosen by God. She was a servant of Abraham's wife, Sarah.

A son was born through Hagar; she named him Ishmael. He became the father of the modern Arab nations. Abraham might have asked himself. If God had promised him a son from which He would make a great nation, where was the son?

He was old, and Sarah was also an older woman. How could it be possible, and where would a son come from? I believe God encouraged him by saying, **"I am a miracle-working God."**

If Sarah is 90 years old, I can still make her young with a new womb to carrying a child. What God did in this situation can be a great reassurance to us today. God can make a miracle, and no one can create miracles as He can!

Abraham Believed in God:

The Bible reveals to us that Abraham believed in God and what He told him. Finally, the miracles of God came to pass, and Sarah delivered a son whom Abraham called Isaac.

And then another test of faith came toward Abraham. When God called for him to sacrifice his son of promise as an offering to the Lord. Abraham took his son Isaac to the top of Mount Moriah to make a sacrifice to God.

When the hour came, they were ready to make an offering on the altar. Abraham was preparing to kill his son; God knew He had tested his faith. He provided a ram nearby for Abraham, which caught in a thicket.

This is an outstanding picture of how God would sacrifice His only Son for the sins of the world. The Word of God tells us that Abraham was considered a friend of God.

"But you, Israel, are My servant, Jacob whom I have chosen, The descendants of Abraham My friend." Isaiah 41:8, NKJV.

The Story of Isaac

ISAAC BECAME A MAN and was growing under the blessing of his father, Abraham. God wanted Isaac to become a man of the covenant for the fulfillment of God's plan.

Abraham instructed him on how to live a good life of prosperity, wealth, and faith. When Isaac became older to a certain age, and his father thought to find a wife for him. So, Abraham directed his servant for traveling to another region to find a wife for Isaac.

Abraham's servant found a good wife and brought Rebekah back with him. Isaac saw them approaching from afar; he saw Rebekah was with the servant.

He went toward them, and he loved Rebekah very much. Isaac became forty years old when he got married to his cousin Rebekah.

Isaac had Two Sons:

I believe Abraham had taught Isaac to have faith. He learned to have an experience with God and to follow God's law.

The Bible says that Isaac was truly blessed with enormous possessions. Then, the other nations around were jealous of him. Isaac begins to have a family when Rebekah gave birth to twin sons, Jacob and Esau.

Isaac loved Esau, and when he was becoming old, he decided to give him the birthright blessing because Esau was the older brother. But Rebekah loved Jacob and wanted to favor him.

She helped to deceive Isaac, tricking him into passing on the blessing to Jacob rather than Esau. When Esau discovered that he had lost the blessing from his father, he tried to kill Jacob.

Rebekah made arrangements to send Jacob away to her brother Laban far in another country. So that he could stay there until everything became peaceful again.

Famine in the Land:

There was a famine that started in the land, but the Lord took care of Isaac and his whole household. God told him not to move down to Egypt, but to stay where he was in the land.

He would continue to provide and to prosper all his household and keep them safe from famine. We will learn next about the man who was chosen by God, Jacob.

He would continue to carry and uphold Abraham's covenant. God's chosen generation will move forward by the sovereign plan of God.

The encouraging word is that the hand of God upon Isaac is now passed on to Jacob's lines. God's glory will continue to be the people of Israel.

After Isaac died at 180 years old, both of his sons mourned their father. God's promise was established from one descendant to the next by the direction of God.

"So Isaac breathed his last and died, and was gathered to his people, being old and full of days. And his sons Esau and Jacob buried him." Genesis 35:29, NKJV.

The Story of Jacob

LET'S LOOK FURTHER AT Jacob's way of life and knowing about his struggles and his challenges. He realized that he was going through a journey of upholding Abraham's covenant with God.

Jacob's confidence truly inspires us. He chose to follow God's blessings in his life. As we continue, we can see he is becoming a stronger and more hardworking man. He was experiencing the abundant blessings of God.

Jacob's name means "deceiver." When his mother was pregnant with Jacob and his brother, Esau. God spoke to Rebekah and told her that she was carrying twin sons in her womb.

God makes these two brothers who would come out as two nations. But the older son would one day serve the other younger son. Esau had a passion for hunting, but Jacob stayed in with his mother and helped around the fields.

Jacob Received the Birthright:

Isaac was getting old, wanted to bless Esau for giving him the birthright. But his mother didn't want Isaac to give him the blessing. She made a plan to trick Isaac to give a birthright blessing to Jacob.

After Isaac blessed Jacob and then Esau discovered that Jacob had deceived him. Esau found out that he lost his blessings from his father. He thought to prepare a plan to kill Jacob later.

So, Jacob escaped by the direction of his mother, Rebekah, to move to a far land to his uncle's house, Laban.

Hard Working for Marriage:

During his journey to the land of Haran, before he arrived at his uncle Laban's house, Jacob had a dream. He saw a ladder rising to heaven with God at the top and angels ascending and descending on the ladder.

Jacob named the place **"Bethel."** The meaning of Bethel is the **"House of God."** Jacob preferred to serve God. He started to work for Laban for seven years because he loved Rachel.

He worked hard to establish a family and serve God. He has such favor on Jacob, and God began blessing the house of Laban as well.

After seven years of hard work, Jacob was expecting to receive Rachel as a wife. But her father, Laban, deceived Jacob on the night of the wedding. He placed another daughter, Leah, in the wedding room for Jacob.

When Jacob found out what had happened to him. Laban made another proposal for Jacob to work for seven years again to take Rachel as a wife. He succeeded, and he loved Rachel more than Leah.

Jacob' Sons:

When Jacob realized that God was His true Father. He experienced that God was still with him; he trusted God.

From this story, we can learn and apply in our lives that when we learn our lesson, and we must then move on to the next challenge of life.

Jacob had six children with Leah; these sons' names were **Reuben, Simeon, Levi, Judah, Issachar, and Zebulun.** Leah had one daughter named **Dinah.**

Rachel was barren for many years, but finally, God blessed her with two sons: **Joseph and Benjamin.** Jacob's wife Rachel died while she gave birth to Benjamin.

Leah had two concubines, *Bilhah and Zilpah*.

Bilhah also had two sons named **Dan and Naphtali**.

Zilpah also had two sons named **Gad and Asher.**

So, since Jacob had twelve sons, they became the twelve tribes of Israel.

Two Brothers Reconciled:

Jacob had a threat to his life from his own brother that went on for a long time, from when he had stolen Esau's birthright for himself.

Jacob knew that his brother would come someday in the future to kill him. He will take all his family and his possessions away from him.

Eventually, his brother, Esau, sent a message to Jacob that he was coming to see him. Before his arrival, Jacob was alone with God. I believe he was praying all night long, wrestling with angels, pleading for mercy.

He was asking for protection from God. He desperately needed God's blessing from the angels. Finally, the angels gave up and asked him, "What is your name?" He replied, **"Jacob."**

They replied, "Your name will not be Jacob, but will be "**Israel."** Because you're wrestling with angels."

Jacob called the place **"Peniel,"** which means he had seen God. The Lord had spared his life. Finally, Jacob and his brother Esau reconciled with each other.

Fulfill God's Plan:

God doesn't look at any of our weaknesses or mistakes. Despite Jacob's fault, he believed God that He had called him to become a leader.

God used him to fulfill His plan on the earth. He is looking at our strong faith to declare God's name that we become a witness of His glory.

The encouraging word here is that God can use anybody, anywhere, to establish His plan on the earth.

The Story of Joseph

THE LESSON WE CAN learn today through the dynamic story of Joseph. It would teach us that, no matter if everyone turns against us. But God is beside us, and He makes way for us.

The story of Joseph's life began when he was seventeen years old, working as a shepherd in his father's flock. He loved to be out there serving his family.

His father, Jacob, loved him very much. His mother, Rachel, had passed away at the time of Benjamin's birth.

Jacob loved Joseph so much that he gave him a coat with many colors. But his brothers became very jealous of Joseph because he shared his dream with his family.

Joseph said that someday in the future, they would bow down to him. So, they worked to find a way to destroy his life, to make fun of him. His brothers started to make a plan to kill him in the field, but he trusted his family.

Planned to Kill Joseph:

On that day, one of his brothers, Judah, suggested throwing Joseph into a pit, and they decided to do so. His oldest brother, Reuben, though maybe he could come back and rescue him later.

The other brothers saw that the merchants from Egypt were passing by and on their way back to Egypt. So, they sold Joseph as a slave to these merchants. They took Joseph as a slave into the land of Egypt.

When Reuben came later to rescue his brother, it was too late. The brothers all went to their father and told him what had happened to Joseph.

They made up some story that the wild animals had killed Joseph in the field. They took Joseph's coat that Jacob had given to Joseph and covered it with animal blood to cover up. Jacob deeply mourned over his lost son and cried out for his life.

Joseph Arrived in Egypt:

The encouraging word here is that Joseph never gave up on his faith. Especially since he held on his dream, even though he was taken away to live in a foreign country. He could not depend on his father, Jacob, anymore to protect him.

Now, he lived in a different environment, and he kept his faith and looked up to God as his Father. The Egyptian merchants arrived in Egypt and sold him to a high-ranking local named Potiphar.

Joseph became a supervisor for his master and in charge of his household. Potiphar trusted him in all his household activities. Joseph was very talented in his marvelous work daily. So, Potiphar's wife tried to seduce him, but he refused her.

He tried to escape from her, not to be trapped. He knew this temptation was not from God. It doesn't honor the God of Israel to tempt him, and so he fled. She accused him of false allegations to Potiphar, who he put Joseph in jail.

Joseph in Jail:

When I think about it, Joseph was a faithful man to serve his master in his house. He made the right thing in the sight of Almighty God to please Him. In this kind of situation, what can we do to fix the problem?

Joseph was also blessed when he was spending his time in prison. According to the Word of God, Joseph was an innocent man in prison for about thirteen years. Two men were convicted from the Pharaoh palace, put them into prison along with Joseph.

They shared their dreams with him, and Joseph interpreted the dreams for them. One of these men was the cupbearer of Pharaoh's palace. Joseph interpreted his dream for him; then, after a while, he got released from prison.

Joseph interpreted Pharaoh's Dream:

Two years later, the Pharaoh had a dream, but he couldn't find anyone to interpret and give him the meaning of the dream. His cupbearer remembered a man, Joseph, in prison who had helped him to interpret his dream.

He told Pharaoh about Joseph. Pharaoh asked him to come to his palace to help his dream. Joseph came in the presence of the Pharaoh. He interpreted the Pharaoh's dream. It means; there would be seven years of plentiful harvest, after which seven years of famine would take place.

Joseph advised them to start to store all the grain and crops so that they could survive the next seven years of famine. When Pharaoh couldn't find any wise man to handle and control all of the goods in the storehouse.

He decided to put Joseph in charge of all things, and Joseph became the second in command of authority in Egypt.

The Famine Started:

The famine started and drastically affected the land of Canaan. Jacob and his family had to do everything to survive in the time of famine. Jacob sent his sons to Egypt to get some grain and food because nothing could be found except in Egypt.

All of Jacob's sons traveled the long journey to Egypt, except for Benjamin. They tried seeking for food, so they brought the case to Joseph's attention that some people came from some foreign lands. Even from the land of Canaan, to get grain and food.

Joseph recognized them for who they were, but he claimed that Egyptian soldiers had accused them of spying. Joseph had planned an idea for his brothers; they couldn't recognize him.

Joseph told them to bring in the younger brother. He would keep one of their brothers, Simon, until they came back. Joseph had not yet identified himself to them as who he was.

All the brothers went back to Jacob, who was mourning over losing Joseph and Simon all over again. Jacob allowed Benjamin to go with them to Egypt to show that they were not spies, that they had only come for grain and food.

Joseph's Brother Came Back:

Joseph found out that his brothers had arrived. They had come with their brother Benjamin, just as Joseph had ordered. Simon would be released and rejoined with his brothers.

Joseph ordered a gathering with a good meal before he showed up to the room to meet them. He saw then that his own brother, Benjamin, had come with them.

He came out of his chamber, and when they all bowed down to him, the prophecy was fulfilled.

"And when Joseph came home, they brought him the present which was in their hand into the house, and bowed down before him to the earth." Genesis 43:26, NKJV.

Knowing Changed hearts:

Joseph still wanted to know that his brothers' hearts had been changed. Did they become men, or were they the same characters? He tested them, and he ordered them to put their money in their sacks; they put a silver cup in Benjamin's sack.

When they were on the way, leaving out of Egypt. Joseph ordered the men to go after them to bring Benjamin back to him. When they found out they had a silver cup in Benjamin's sack, they accused him of stealing.

Joseph said, "I will keep him here so that you may go back to your home country." Even though Judah had begged him not to keep Benjamin; if he wanted to do so. It might be their father Jacob would die.

Joseph Revealed Himself:

Finally, Joseph revealed himself to his brothers. Joseph wept with them and told them.

"Then Joseph could not restrain himself before all those who stood by him, and he cried out, "Make everyone go out from me!"

So no one stood with him while Joseph made himself known to his brothers. And he wept aloud, and the Egyptians and the house of Pharaoh heard it." Genesis 45:1-3, NKJV.

Joseph instructed them to go back home and to bring his father, along with all his household, back to Egypt.

They went to their father's home, and they brought Jacob along with all his family to Egypt. After many years Jacob met Joseph, and he settled down there, the rest of his life until he died.

We learn here that although they did for evil, God turned it around for good. We must desire to look up and focus on the God of Israel, knowing that He is surrounding us with His grace and mercy.

"But as for you, you meant evil against me; but God meant it for good, in order to bring it about as it is this day, to save many people alive." Genesis 50:20, NKJV.

The Story of Moses

WE WOULD LIKE TO learn about Moses' life and how the Lord God had chosen him out of millions of Jewish people. They were all slaves in Egypt under Pharaoh's authority.

When God chooses someone willing to do the work of God. There will not any doubt in my mind that He wants to use an ordinary person for the right task. He prepares him for a great assignment in the Kingdom of God.

This is an encouraging word for us that God will choose those who can handle the work of God. He gives us the ability with a fresh anointing to carry His strategy to the best of our knowledge. He knows our hearts, and that we can make the plan of God.

Moses's Childhood:

Let's look at Moses' childhood. He was born into a Jewish family of all slaves who were working hard to survive. So, at the time of Moses' birth, a new Pharaoh ordered that any newborn male born to a Hebrew woman would be killed so that he would not grow up.

The mother of Moses sought to save Moses' life. She realized that there was a purpose to Moses' life. She put her baby Moses into a basket on the river Nile. On that day and at the right time when the daughter of Pharaoh was in the water.

The princess saw that there was a basket coming toward her. When she got the basket, she saw there was a baby in the basket. She adopted the baby and took care of him. Moses grew up in the palace with the lifestyle of the Pharaoh.

No Attention to His Childhood:

When we study this story, it is encouraging to us that Moses paid no attention to his childhood's luxury palace. He had lived at a young age with a good lifestyle.

But he gave up all of his desire for the sake of His people to follow God's plan. He recognized there was a better life ahead of him. Sometimes we may feel that God has more projects and more blessings for us.

It is just a matter of time, and we will eventually get there. God has already made the perfect connection, provisions, and good health for us to be able to live and to serve Him. Glory to His name.

Moses Saw Hardship:

Moses saw the suffering and the hardship of the Jewish people. How the Egyptians had mistreated them. Moses grew and became an adult. One day he saw how an Egyptian was hurting a Jewish worker. He involved himself in the situation; he killed the soldier.

He was so frightened about the incident that he ran away to escape into the land of Midian. There, he met the family of Jethro, who eventually he gave Moses his daughter Zipporah for marriage.

"When Pharaoh heard of this matter, he sought to kill Moses. But Moses fled from the face of Pharaoh and dwelt in the land of Midian, and he sat down by a well." Exodus 2:15, NKJV.

Moses lived there with his wife for forty years. Moses could remember all the times when his people were suffering under Pharaoh's regime in Egypt. He needed to do something about it.

I believe he started to seek the God of his forefathers as he had been taught in his childhood. He knew God could redeem the people. He was searching for God's way to rescue His people in Egypt.

Seeking God is a wonderful way to know Him. God would bring a miracle and will be involved in any situation. When we ask Him, we find Him?

Moses talks with God:

Moses was seeking Him, seeking an alive encounter with God. Finally, God heard and answered his prayer. God instructed him to come up to the top of the mountain to meet with Him.

What a powerful visitation that would have been! Moses got a call to meet with God. He had a great experience with a burning bush up on the mountain. God appeared to him, going to set His people free.

The Lord said that I heard the cry of all the Jewish people in Egypt. Now He had chosen Moses to go back to Egypt, and He would increase his faith to meet with Pharaoh. God told him,

"So the Lord said to Moses: "See, I have made you as God to Pharaoh, and Aaron your brother shall be your prophet. You shall speak all that I command you. And Aaron your brother shall tell Pharaoh to send the children of Israel out of his land." Exodus 7:1-2, NKJV.

God sent Moses to Pharaoh:

This is a good encouraging word. We can learn from the obedience of Moses. He acknowledged God's truth, and he knew that God existed. He was relying on God's promise to be with him to deliver a message to Pharaoh.

God desired to set His people free after four hundred years of slavery and suffering. Moses decided to make the journey to Egypt and found his family and his brother, Aaron.

They stood up with the big challenge to go to the palace of Pharaoh and deliver a message from God. Pharaoh recognized Moses, and the two men spoke boldly to Pharaoh that God wanted to deliver His people from Egypt.

Moses said, **"Let my people go to worship their God."** Pharaoh rejected his request, and God sent ten plagues as a judgment upon the land. Finally, Pharaoh gave in and allowed the Jewish people to be set free from the land of Egypt.

Free to Worship God:

The encouragement here that we can experience is that when we are ready to get free from the bondage of suffering, sins, and darkness,

God has His own way to make it possible for us to be set free. God is restoring our life back to us more than we ever had it before.

He is able to do all things in His name. Now we look at, in the time of Exodus, that Moses received instruction from God. To build a Tabernacle that people would assemble in a tent to worship God.

They brought the Ark of Covenant as a symbol of God's presence among the people. Then the high priest was to perform the annual atonement for the children of Israel.

God provided better guidelines to obtain purity and holiness in the sight of God and how to worship God.

God saw that the people were still disobedient, and God had allowed them to stay in the wilderness for forty years. They were very close to the Land of Promise, but God did not allow Moses to enter the Promised Land.

Wilderness Experience:

God had a plan to prepare Moses and all the Israelites to listen and obey God's command. The nations of Israel were living in the wilderness for forty years to learn to be submissive unto God.

Moses developed a humble spirit to get ready to serve God. I know that Moses struggled in his faith; maybe he had doubt and failure. But he had great courage to move forward because God told him to do so.

Moses recognized God's presence at His performing, what God said would happen. God's timing is extremely important. We must allow God to be the Lord of Miracles. And we wait upon Him and get ready to see His impossible wonders done in His name.

The encouraging word here is that God finished working in the life of Moses. God is now searching our hearts to mold us and make us into the people of God.

Trusting and have faith in Him, and those who are ready to serve and minister to unreached people in our time.

Moses Received Responsibilities:

Moses had an overwhelming responsibility for over two million Israelites who were all expecting to enter the land.

They were waiting to settle down in new homes and build their lives in the land of milk and honey. Some of them complained and brought all of their problems to Moses. But he couldn't solve all of them.

So, his father-in-law, Jethro, advised him to choose some men of God and create a team of elders who would have the responsibilities of taking care of the people

"Moreover you shall select from all the people able men, such as fear God, men of

truth, hating covetousness; and place such over them to be rulers of thousands, rulers of hundreds, rulers of fifties, and rulers of tens." Exodus 18:21, NKJV.

Moses did so—and he began to do another thing, as well. He was ready to listen to God's voice, to go up the mountain, and receive something from the Lord.

"The Ten Commandments":

God told him to come up to the top of the mountain to meet Him again, and he went up there to see God. There was a plan that God had to write out, *the Ten Commandments.*

As the law of God for the new nation of Israel. God wanted to establish a chosen people with a new nation for Himself. So, God shall be exalted and honored by His own people forever.

Moses Finished the Task:

We learn through this story that God might have considered someone else to enter the Promised Land. The Word says that God did not allow Moses to enter the Holy Land.

Moses was recognized as the commander and leader of the Israelites. God had chosen the one who had brought His people out from Egyptian bondage.

We read in the Word that God showed the Promised Land to him from a far distance. I believe that Moses was waiting and dreaming to see the land that he had fought for so many years.

But God and Moses were standing on the mountain. He said, I would show it to you; you will be allowed to see it, but you will not enter the land.

I have assigned another person, Joshua, to carry out the task of taking My people to the Promised Land. Then the Lord said to him.

"This is the land of which I swore to give Abraham, Isaac, and Jacob, saying, 'I will give it to your descendants.' I have caused you to see it with your eyes, but you shall not cross over there." Deuteronomy 34:4, NKJV.

Then, meanwhile, Moses was up on the mountain of Moab with God, he died. The Word says that God buried him up there in Moab. He was 120 years old.

"And He buried him in a valley in the land of Moab, opposite Beth Peor; but no one knows his grave to this day." Deuteronomy 34:6, NKJV.

The Story of Joshua

I AM SHARING A short story of Joshua, who was Moses's assistant in a time of crisis. He had started a walk of faith and serving God with Moses in his youth.

He had a challenging time in his long journey from the day of the Exodus. It became a big struggle to arrive in the land of Canaan.

He was a true person, serving and learning alongside Moses to lead the children of Israel and guide them into the Promised Land. God chose him in his youth, and was very trustworthy and submissive under the authority of Moses.

He recognized Moses' ministry as a leader whom God had appointed to serve the people. He realized that God had taken them away from the hardship of their life of slavery into the Promised Land and a new glorious life in God.

Faithful in his Young Age:

As we know, Joshua was very faithful in his younger age, growing up and helping alongside Moses. I believe that it transferred the anointing of the leadership of Moses onto him to become a great leader.

Moses passed away, and God had chosen Joshua to lead the Israelites into the Promised Land. It is a tremendous responsibility to guide people in the right direction, according to God's plan.

When God calls us, He will be responsible for preparing the way for us and guiding our steps. The Lord said to Joshua: **Be strong and courageous.**

"Have I not commanded you? Be strong and of good courage; do not be afraid, nor be dismayed, for the Lord your God is with you wherever you go." Joshua 1:9, NKJV.

Obeying His Command:

We will study a dynamic word of encouragement from the book of Joshua. Let's look at what happened and why God commanded them to have the word of faith.

The Lord told them to obey His Word. In this situation, they were moving on their journey without direction where they must go.

God began to show up in their lives to direct them to look upon Him. It is written, **"Have I not commanded you?"**

Joshua with a Great Faith:

God gave Joshua a great faith to trust God's authority and observe the command of the Lord God. We see that the anointing of Moses passed on to Joshua, and that's why he turned into a great warrior.

God has fulfilled His promise that they would enter God's Holy Land and step into His blessings. God had directed them to be strong and courageous, not to be afraid.

This is a very encouraging word that God has established everything that would happen in the future.

We all desire to have protection and to be guided by His Spirit. God instructed them not to worship any other gods, only to trust in Him, and look to the God of Israel.

He Trusted God:

God equipped Joshua and instructed him both on the battlefield and in the time of spiritual warfare and crisis. He should trust in the God of Israel and the God of Abraham.

Moses needed to find out what was going on the other side of the land. So that he could have his people move forward and enter the land of milk and honey. He asked for twelve spies to check out the situation.

He didn't want to risk the lives of the people who were living in the desert with no home. But the people were expecting to establish a new home and to build up a unique future for themselves.

Story of Praise Report:

As we remembered, about twelve spies went into the land; ten of those spies came back to give a bad report to Moses. They said they had seen that the enemy were giants and could not be defeated.

But two spies, Joshua and Caleb, came back to give a praise report by faith. They had a strong belief that God will possess the land and had already handed it over to the Children of Israel. Moses believed them.

They took the word of promise and led the people into the land of Canaan. Many enemies came to attack them, but God was behind all the movement to fulfill His promise from the beginning! He is a faithful God.

Joshua in the Battlefield:

Joshua was a warrior in the battlefield against the Amalekites, and when Moses called on the name of God. He called for Joshua to come to fight against the enemy.

Moses lifted his hands up to heaven. He held his hands up for a long hour that God would give them strength and courage prevailed upon the enemy. Joshua helped him to lift his hands to heaven to receive help from the Lord.

"And so it was, when Moses held up his hand, that Israel prevailed; and when he let down his hand, Amalek prevailed." Exodus 17:11, NKJV.

An extraordinary miracle of God took place on that battlefield. The sun stood still, but they continued the fight and conquered the enemy with the victory until they defeated them.

Joshua walked in the sight of God to get ready in war and not be afraid of any opposition.

Crushing the Wall of Jericho:

Joshua had the gift of leadership to be able to listen to God's voice and lead God's people into a glorious future. He determined that God wanted him to cross the Jordan River and march around the city of Jericho for seven days.

Then the last day, they blasted the trumpet and shouted with a loud voice to crush the wall and enter the city.

This was part of God's command that He had given to Joshua. Let's look at Joshua's confidence and trust. He walked by faith and received training through Moses, and he was very faithful in the sight of God.

Moses especially trusted him and gave him the assignment to do the work. We see that crushing a massive wall is a picture of a big mountain, which could be a huge problem and crisis in our own lives.

He had no Doubt:

In this situation, Joshua had faith with no doubt that they could move the big mountain of the Jericho wall. He could have said, "it doesn't make any sense, this wall has built by materials of concrete and stone."

There is no way to crush this wall by marching and shouting with all the warriors for victory. But he believed the word, and he trusted the name of the God of Israel who had promised to take them into a wonderful future.

He didn't consider the things that man would see as impossible. He experienced that all things were possible with almighty God.

God is Bigger than our Problems:

It might be that our own human thought will not solve the problem of our Jericho wall. If we are fighting the heavy burden, we cannot crush it through our own power.

God is able to transform what He promises to fulfill for all of us. Joshua experienced a strong faith to believe that everything is possible with God. Our faith and trusting His Word would take us to a high level of glory.

No matter how mighty the mountain or how powerful the wall would be? God is stronger sufficient to demolish them. To make them seem like nothing, and to create something wonderful out of the situation.

Consider the big problems that you have. You must pray and bring all of your crises into His presence. He will release His victory and blessings onto you. You belong to Him, and He is taking care of you because He loves you.

The Story of Judges

WE LEARN SO MANY encouraging words from this book during the formation of the people of Israel. As we read after the death of Joshua, the people would not follow God's law. They wanted to worship other gods.

They turned into idol-worshipers. People rebelled against God and did not want to keep a true attitude in the sight of God.

So, the tribes fought against among themselves and demanded to win the battle for some parts of the land. But they couldn't succeed in the battle without God.

The enemy attacked them, and God brought oppression against Israel to teach them to trust Him. Any time the nation failed to follow the God of Israel, they were defeated, and then they repented their sins.

The nation called on the name of God many times, and God granted them to victory on the battlefield. The bad news is that the people would always continue to worship other gods again.

God raised up twelve judges to deliver the people from the hand of their enemies and to save the nation of Israel. The following people were the warriors and the heroes of faith in the time of transition.

Othniel

The first judge was Othniel, son of Kenaz; he was Caleb's younger brother. God raised up Othniel as a judge and a commander in Israel. He conquered the king of Mesopotamia, and the Israelites experienced peace succeeding in the land.

Othniel's influence extended for a long time, as he continued to go to war for the nations, and they had peace for forty years.

"When the children of Israel cried out to the Lord, the Lord raised up a deliverer for the children of Israel, who delivered them: Othniel the son of Kenaz, Caleb's younger brother.

The Spirit of the Lord came upon him, and he judged Israel. He went out to war, and

the Lord delivered Cushan-Rishathaim king of Mesopotamia into his hand; and his hand prevailed over Cushan-Rishathaim.

So the land had rest for forty years. Then Othniel the son of Kenaz died." Judges 3:9-11, NKJV.

Ehud

The second judge was Ehud, and he was left-handed. After Othniel died, the nations transferred their faith and followed Eglon, the king of Moab. After they had served him for eighteen years, they cried out to God to free them.

Ehud made a sword and slew King Eglon. Ehud fled the scene, and he went to blast a trumpet in the mountain of Ephraim.

He declared to the nation of Israel to **"follow me, for the Lord has given your enemies to you."** The Israelites attacked and massacred about 10,000 men of Moab. They had harmony for the next eighty years.

"Then he said to them, "Follow me, for the Lord has delivered your enemies the Moabites into your hand." So they went down after him, seized the fords of the

Jordan leading to Moab, and did not allow anyone to cross over." Judges 3:28, NKJV.

Shamgar

The third judge was Shamgar, about whom we have no details of his life. There is only one short verse included in the Scriptures about his victory.

The verse tells us that Shamgar was the son of Anath. He attacked six hundred men and killed all the Philistines with an ox goad (generally known as a great stick).

Then he delivered the people. He destroyed the enemies of God's people. There is no record of how many years God allowed him to judge over His people.

"After him was Shamgar the son of Anath, who killed six hundred men of the Philistines with an ox goad; and he also delivered Israel." Judges 3:31, NKJV.

Deborah

The fourth judge was Deborah, the only female judge. She was married to Lapidoth. We will be reviewing the life of Deborah, the female prophetess and judge of Israel.

She had an extraordinary passion for serving and being a leader of the nation in the time of oppression. The people couldn't win the fight because the enemy was stronger than them.

But Deborah was a woman commander to the army of Israelites. She could hear and obey the voice of the Lord when God ordered her to attack Sisera.

"Now Deborah, a prophetess, the wife of Lapidoth, was judging Israel at that time. And she would sit under the palm tree of Deborah between Ramah and Bethel in the mountains of Ephraim. And the children of Israel came up to her for judgment." Judges 4:4-5, NKJV.

Deborah commanded the people to defeat Sisera because God was watching the situation and directing them.

He wanted to show the people how to grow into fearless warriors and to remind them that they were stronger than their enemies. No matter how many armies they had or how powerful their swords and other equipment!

When God told Deborah to move forward by the Spirit of God to kill the giants, they succeeded. They won a great victory on the battlefield.

We learn here that a woman had received the call of God to kill the giant armies of the enemy that all of the others were afraid to attack.

The people could not move forward before the word of command came from Deborah to attack Sisera. Deborah trusted God and made a straightforward call to move out against the enemy.

It might be that we are also afraid in some situations in our lives, but we must move forward to attack the devil. We recognize that the devil is a liar and a deceiver who seeks to destroy every one of us.

Gideon

The fifth judge was Gideon. Let's look at the life of Gideon, as recorded in the Bible. Gideon was a good military man and a leader of the army. He wanted to carry God's mission forth to serve and accomplish a wonderful work for his people.

For seven years, they had experienced many invasions from the Midianites, Amalekites, and other Eastern foreigners in the land. Their enemy had damaged all their crops and cattle.

People had suffered and lost their faith in God. They had begun to worship other gods, but now they cried out to the God of Israel for guidance.

"So Israel was greatly impoverished because of the Midianites, and the children of Israel cried out to the Lord." Judges 6:6, NKJV.

God appointed a prophet to remind the people that those who had forsaken Him in the past. But they should look back that there is a God in heaven.

"Also I said to you, "I am the Lord your God; do not fear the gods of the Amorites, in whose land you dwell." But you have not obeyed My voice." Judges 6:10, NKJV.

Gideon was truly faithful to obey God and to be submissive to the God of Israel. He had a wonderfully close encounter with God, and the fear of God was all over him.

The Bible tells us that Gideon destroyed the idols and all other gods. The people appeared to recognize and worship the One True God again.

Because of his faithfulness and fear of God, Gideon received more blessings. The people request him to be a leader and the Judge over Israel.

The encouraging story and words here can teach us a profound message:

- Gideon was faithful to respond to God.
- Gideon was not a quitter.
- Gideon was obedient to God's call.
- Gideon had a fear of God toward what God told him to do.
- Gideon recognized that God was mighty and great in every situation of life.

Tola

The sixth judge was Tola, the son of Puah. God established his leadership after the death of Abimelech. There is not much information about the life of Tola; he is the least reported judge. There are no recorded actions of Tola. But we do know that he obeyed what God called him to serve.

He was chosen to lead in wisdom and reconciliation for the nations of Israel. He ruled for twenty-three years.

"After Abimelech there arose to save Israel Tola the son of Puah, the son of Dodo, a man of Issachar; and he dwelt in Shamir in the mountains of Ephraim. He judged Israel twenty-three years; and he died and was buried in Shamir." Judges 10:1-2, NKJV.

Jair

The seventh judge was Jair, and only a few verses talk about this judge. The Word says that Jair had thirty sons, and they traveled with a large family to thirty cities riding with thirty donkeys!

This indicates that God allowed thirty peaceful years for Israel during the time when Jair was the judge over the nations. He was a judge and a leader for twenty-two years.

"After him arose Jair, a Gileadite; and he judged Israel twenty-two years. Now he had thirty sons who rode on thirty donkeys; they also had thirty towns, which are called "Havoth Jair" to this day, which are in the land of Gilead. And

Jair died and was buried in Camon." Judges 10:3-5, NKJV.

Jephthah

The eighth judge was Jephthah, who came from Gilead. He was born from a prostitute. He was forced to leave when his brothers threw him out of the house.

Because he was believed to be an improper child, he did not get any inheritance from his family. The Bible indicates that he went to the region of Tob and settled there. He became a mighty fighter.

While there, he gathered a gang of scoundrels around him, and they followed him. He fought in the battle and prevailed. Jephthah was only a judge for six years.

"Gilead's wife bore sons; and when his wife's sons grew up, they drove Jephthah out, and said to him, "You shall have no inheritance in our father's house, for you are the son of another woman."

"Then Jephthah fled from his brothers and dwelt in the land of Tob; and worthless men

banded together with Jephthah and went out raiding with him." Judges 11:2-3, NKJV.

Ibzan

The ninth judge was Ibzan, who had thirty sons and thirty daughters in marriage! He brought in thirty women for his thirty sons! Ibzan served Israel, and God blessed him with many sons and daughters.

He offered his thirty sons and thirty daughters in marriage to those outside of his tribe. As we know, Ibzan was born, and his life ended in the same city. His sixty sons and daughters made enormous changes in his life.

This would have formed many alliances with other Israelites and would have increased his effectiveness as a ruler. He was a judge for seven years. Then Ibzan passed away and was buried in Bethlehem.

"After him, Ibzan of Bethlehem judged Israel. He had thirty sons. And he gave away thirty daughters in marriage, and brought in thirty daughters from elsewhere for his sons. He judged Israel seven years. Then Ibzan died

and was buried at Bethlehem." Judges 12:8-10, NKJV.

Elon

The tenth judge was Elon. We don't have a lot of records about his leadership. He ruled Israel for ten years in his stage of authority, and he was from the tribe of Zebulun. When Elon died, he was buried in Aijalon in the land of Zebulun.

"After him, Elon the Zebulunite judged Israel. He judged Israel ten years. And Elon the Zebulunite died and was buried at Aijalon in the country of Zebulun." Judges 12:11-12, NKJV.

Abdon

The eleventh judge was Abdon, a son of Hillel from Pirathon, who served Israel. God blessed his household with forty sons and thirty grandsons. He was extremely wealthy and had a huge family; they rode on seventy donkeys.

Abdon was from the tribe of Ephraim. He would have been a successful man who was recognized in his day. When Abdon passed away, he was buried at Pirathon in Ephraim in the hill country of the Amalekites. He led Israel for eight years.

"After him, Abdon the son of Hillel the Pirathonite judged Israel. He had forty sons and thirty grandsons, who rode on seventy young donkeys. He judged Israel eight years.

Then Abdon the son of Hillel the Pirathonite died and was buried in Pirathon in the land of Ephraim, in the mountains of the Amalekites." Judges 12:13-15, NKJV.

Samson

The twelfth judge was Samson, and his narrative comes out with the message of his birth. An angel appeared to his father, Manoah, and his wife gave them good news then she gave birth to Samson. The story of Samson is interesting.

He was the toughest man in the Bible, and he ended his own life. He went through the wrong direction, causing him his own death, but he won the victory over his enemies, the Philistines.

God will work even through sinful men to achieve His plans. Samson voluntarily moved into places where he started to sin, but nevertheless, God trusted him for His triumph. Samson was a man of strong bodily power.

The Spirit of God moved upon him in many circumstances, giving him enormous bravery to attack the Philistines. These people were the opposition to the Israelites.

Although Samson was loved the woman Delilah, Samson's story points out that fleshly temptation produces destruction and disobedience.

God uses sinful people to achieve His will by the mercy of God. Samson carried out his assignment as a judge in Israel for twenty years.

"And his brothers and all his father's household came down and took him, and brought him up and buried him between Zorah and Eshtaol in the tomb of his father Manoah. He had judged Israel twenty years." Judges 16:31, NKJV.

Summary of Twelfth Judges:

God has called each of these men and the one woman, and they were all ready to change the nation and bring the people back to God.

People were committing sins against the law of God, but God remembered the covenant He had made with His people through Abraham. He would watch over His people.

The encouraging word here is that God does not want us to be idol-worshipers or to follow other gods. We need to study that the people of Israel were following their own ideas of how to worship other gods to satisfy their lives.

This teaches us that following God requires faith and confidence in His Word and our obedience to His direction and guidance. If we observe His commandments, we will become successful and prosperous people. Amen.

The Book of Ruth

THE STORY OF RUTH is a tragic one; she experienced many hurtful and difficult situations
in her life. And yet we read how God blessed her
because she followed Naomi to Bethlehem. God
even included her in Jesus' ancestry.

There was a famine in the land of Moab.
Naomi was the wife of Elimelech, and they had
two sons. Elimelech died, and these two sons
had wives; one of the sons had a wife named
Orpah; the other son's wife was named Ruth.
After a while, these wives' husbands also died.

Naomi, Orpah, and Ruth needed to get out
of the land of Moab because of a famine. They
were leaving everything behind and going toward Bethlehem.

Naomi had Journey with Ruth:

In the middle of their journey, Naomi
spoke to them to tell them that they were free
to go. She offered them to leave wherever they

wanted, and if they both wished to go back to their homeland.

Orpah decided to go back alone by herself in her own way. But Ruth said to her mother-in-law, "I will go nowhere, but wherever you go, I will go with you."

But Ruth said:

"Entreat me not to leave you,

Or to turn back from following after you;

For wherever you go, I will go;

And wherever you lodge, I will lodge;

Your people shall be my people,

And your God, my God.

Where you die, I will die,

And there will I be buried.

The Lord do so to me, and more also,

If anything but death parts you and me."

Ruth 1:16-18, NKJV.

When Naomi realized that she made her mind with a strong determination to go with her. She stayed quiet to speak with her. They traveled to Bethlehem together. When they arrived there, they went to meet a man who was a relative of Naomi.

He was very wealthy, and his name was Boaz. Ruth asked Naomi if she should go to the field to work. The owner of the field was very rich. He saw that there was a woman who was working hard to glean food, grain in the field.

Boaz asked who the woman was? He was told that it was Ruth who had come from Moab. Ruth received the favor of God. Boaz had allowed her to work in his fields.

"So Boaz took Ruth and she became his wife; and when he went in to her, the Lord gave her conception, and she bore a son." Ruth 4:13, NKJV.

Ruth and Boaz Married:

In this romantic story of Ruth and Boaz, God prepared a way for them to meet each other in the field. Boaz met Ruth, and they got married, and they had a son named Obed.

He was the father of Jesse, and Jesse was the father of King David. Ruth turned into part of the family line of King David and ultimately of Jesus Himself.

Ruth had no idea what was coming up in her day. We don't have any reports about Ruth's family. Why she didn't go the other way or go back to her own family when Naomi offered to release her.

But Ruth had the heart to be submissive to Naomi and follow her mother-in-law; she even said, **"Wherever you go, I will go."**

Inspiring Words:

Let's review here for encouraging words from a wonderful story. It is a story about coming from nothing to have something great happen in the life of Ruth. She was able to pass on a mighty blessing to the next generations to come.

God was in control of the lives of everyone who was involved in this story. God wanted to be recognized, and the people were also seeking God's blessing to help them.

Can we say to the Lord also, **"Lord, wherever You go, I will follow You"**? What a great picture, and what a blessing it would be if we could give this beautiful testimony in our lives for the glory of God.

We must be ready to trust the Lord, and no matter what situation we are in, He is able to make way for us.

The Story of Samuel

IN THIS STORY, THERE are many wonderful, encouraging words to help us learn our passions in serving God. Let's look at Samuel's mother, Hannah. She was barren, but even though she thought she couldn't have any child.

Hannah did not give up on crying out to the God of Israel for a child. Samuel's mother interceded for her new child, even though Samuel was not yet born. Hannah even prophesied that her son would become a powerful prophet of the nation.

Hannah had a passion and having the desire to seek God in the Temple. She was searching for the answer to establishing a future of God's servant Samuel. She even asked to dedicate her son to the Lord.

Samuel grew up with the wonderful capability to listen to God. There is always a word that can capture our spiritual attention to the Word of God.

Thus, the Word can build us up and bring us into the great fruit of the Spirit of God. We will learn this powerful story about Samuel, the first prophet of Israel.

Hannah Sought God:

Hannah was in the Temple, pursuing God, but her search for God was very astonishing. As she was crying out to God, Eli, the priest, said to her, "Hannah, are you drunk?" She said, *"No, my lord. I am pouring out my heart to my God for an answer."*

God answered her prayer with a son to Hannah, and she gave him the name of Samuel, which means *"hears of God."* We have no record of how old Samuel was when his mother, Hannah, dedicated him to the Lord in the Temple.

As he grew up, he learned through hearing the Word and being submissive under Eli, the priest. Samuel flourished under the anointing of the Lord. God chose him to carry out the ministry of prophecy in the land of Israel.

Samuel was a boy, but God called him to serve the Lord. He didn't even know God, and he did not recognize God's voice at first. But he wanted to follow God's plan for his life.

Samuel, Hearing God's Voice:

Let's look at Samuel's childhood life: He started to receive a call of God and to get connected to Eli, who was a priest in the house of God. So, God directed his life into a magnificent ministry in Israel.

I love how God called Samuel while he was sleeping. The Lord woke him up, and the young boy thought Eli was calling him. So, he went to the older priest. Eli said, *"I didn't call you. Go back to sleep until the morning time."*

Eli then told Samuel that if he heard the voice of God again, he should say, "Speak. My Lord, your servant is listening," ***"Now the Lord came and stood and called as at other times, Samuel! Samuel!"*** 1 Samuel 3:10, NKJV.

God taught Samuel about faith, dreams, and visions. He gave him a message of judgment to relate to Eli's family, including his sons. Samuel's name and his reputation spread throughout the land.

Samuel had two sons of his own, and they were walking with God. Israel had no king yet, and Samuel wanted to appoint his son as a king, but Samuel was advised not to do so.

Samuel Anointed King Saul:

They were demanding that Samuel appoint another king for Israel. So, the Lord decided Saul to become the first king of Israel.

"Then Samuel took a flask of oil and poured it on his head, and kissed him and said: "Is it not because the Lord has anointed you commander over His inheritance?" 1 Samuel 10:1, NKJV.

When Saul had reigned over Israel a while, he became disobedient against God. Later, Samuel told Saul that God had rejected him. And Samuel said to Saul. God instructed Samuel to appoint another king for Israel, which was David.

"You have done foolishly. You have not kept the commandment of the Lord your God, which He commanded you. For now, the Lord would

have established your kingdom over Israel forever." 1 Samuel 13:13, NKJV.

Encouraging Words:

In the encouraging stories told here, we learn
how to apply to our Christian life that when we
hear the voice of God. He will prepare us and
take us into the assignment that He has already
chosen for us.

Because God will call us into His sovereign
plan, and we will speak His name and proclaim
His Word.

For me to receive a call from God is an honor.
It is a privilege to dedicate my life and humbling
myself to the plan of God. Are you ready to hear
the Lord?

He gives us directions on how to serve! Do
you need to know what the next step for you
is? Seek Him; He will be found. I believe He is
calling anyone who will lay down his life for the
Lord, and they shall be rewarded for eternity.

The Story of David

THIS POWERFUL STORY COMFORTS us and encourages us through the life and ministry of David. We look back to when God appointed a servant to be sent out into enormous challenges of life.

But we see that God is reigning over many generations in the land of Israel. Every word of God has a meaning and a purpose of something greater than we can imagine. We may, later, understand the meaning of the word.

We desire that the Word will restore us and help us to experience Him better. For David, it wasn't easy to move up to the next level of accomplishment. But there will always be difficulties in life and also living a good time.

David had a huge burden, trying to get out of all the problems of life and move into fulfilling his future. I think we all have happy times and confusing times.

David also had those kinds of feelings and doubts. But he determined to go on to get greater levels of wisdom and knowledge in God.

Faithful in His Father's Field:

At that time, he didn't recognize what God had in store for him. Gradually, the plan of God revealed to his life. He didn't notice what God had chosen him to do for His people in the land of Israel. As a boy in the fields, he took care of his father's flocks.

David just wanted to do his father's work, what he was instructed to do. He wished to be obedient to his father's house.

Studying about David; he was a faithful man even as a boy in the field, which was a calm place for him to be! He understood how to be sincere to learn in his small field.

The encouraging word here is that David chose to serve God, and his heart was right in the sight of God.

The Word of God says that if you are faithful with small things. He will see what you accomplish, and God will increase your assignments.

He will bring in more tasks for us to carry in the work of God.

David Anointed as a King:

As we learned, Samuel had a strong encounter with God. He realized that God had decided to bring another king to the nation of Israel. God sent Samuel to the house of Jesse, the father of David, to choose the next king.

On the day of Samuel's plan, to arrive at Jesse's house. Samuel looked around among Jesse's sons to identify the chosen one whom God had already appointed. He came to anoint the elected man as the next king of Israel.

Samuel didn't have peace in his heart that any of these sons was the one whom God wanted! And so, Samuel asked Jesse if he had any other sons, and if so, would he bring them to him?

Jesse said, "Yes, I have a young boy who is in the field taking care of the flocks at the moment." Samuel asked him to bring David; then, he arrived in the presence of Samuel.

The prophet recognized that he was the one God whom he had chosen to become the next king of Israel after King Saul. Samuel took the anointing oil, and he poured it over David's head. I believe he decreed, David should be the next king of Israel.

God Prepared David:

When David was a young boy, God had set things up to prepare him. The Lord needed to teach him to direct his life.

The Lord taught him to grow and mature in life. When God calls us into His kingdom, it doesn't mean we are already ready prepared the very next day to serve Him.

He develops our character and personality into a humble vessel of honor for Himself first. It may take months and maybe years to get prepared before God trusts us to send us out into a great ministry.

Throughout the books of Samuel, we learn about the life of David. He went through disappointment and discouragement and many crises in his life. He even received a death threat made by King Saul.

David Killed the Giant:

Samuel passed away before David became the king of Israel. God raised up Nathan to serve as the next prophet in Israel. David went into the battle alongside King Saul. You may have heard about the enemy that was attacking Israel on the battlefield, the Philistines.

The Israelites army couldn't kill the giant enemy, Goliath, who was nine feet tall. Everyone was afraid, and they didn't know how to get rid of him. They were trying not to get killed.

David went there, and when he got to the front lines, he picked up his slingshot that held five stones. He pulled a shot into Goliath's forehead. The giant fell down on the ground, and David cut off his head.

It was great news of victory around the land. David became very popular because of his brave action. King Saul became very jealous of him, to the point that he planned to kill David.

King Saul had a son, Jonathan; he was very close friends with David. King Saul had disobeyed God. The Lord had rejected King Saul, declaring that his kingdom would come to an end. King Saul died on the battlefield.

David as a King:

There will always be serious consequences when we disobey God and go our own way. We may understand that King David made mistakes, but God forgave him because he loved God. We read in the Word that David was described as *"the man after God's own heart."*

"But now your kingdom shall not continue. The Lord has sought for Himself *a man after His own heart*, and the Lord has commanded him to be commander over His people, because you have not kept what the Lord commanded you." 1 Samuel 13:14, NKJV.

David took over his own tribe of Judah for seven years, staying in the city of Hebron. Afterward, he took over the northern and southern tribes, and the twelve tribes were under his authority.

David had the ambition to bring the Ark of Covenant back to Israel. Palestine had captured the Ark. Later on, David's son King Solomon built the Temple for God.

Finally, when they brought the Ark back, David danced on that day because he was so glad that the Ark had come back home. David had the heart to build up a Temple of God.

"Go and tell My servant David, 'Thus says the Lord: "Would you build a house for Me to dwell in?" 2 Samuel 7:5, NKJV.

David fallen into Sins:

As we study in the Word of God from the life of David, and he fell away in sins and adultery. But David recognized the temptation in his life. He realized that something was wrong.

We all are going into many different temptations that can become out of control in our lives. No matter how we worship and to serve God.No matter how we worship and to serve God.

The Lord sees our weaknesses and strengths in our lives. Sometimes our temptations get us into trouble. Of course, Nathan came to David to warn him that he had sinned against God by having adultery with Bathsheba and killing her husband, Uriah.

David repented and cried out for the mercy of God. He did not lose the heart of God, but he sought Him with all of his heart. Later on, Bathsheba became pregnant by David, and God brought judgment upon him because he had sinned against God.

As a result, they lost their child. David had sons, and one of his sons was Solomon. Nathan anointed Solomon as the next king of Israel. David reigned and ruled as king over Israel for forty years and died at the age of seventy.

Encouragement Words:

Let's look at this story to pick up a word of encouragement from it. Despite David's faults and his sin and his disobedience against God. But God has not removed His covenant from him.

We can learn from the Word of God and to apply David's experiences to our lives today. God expects us to be faithful and obedient to Him. Loving God with all our soul, mind, and heart.

If we do all these things and God knows everything about us. His grace shall be sufficient for us every day. God is faithful, and He requires us to be truthful to Him.

The Story of Solomon

STUDYING THE STORY OF Solomon would be a good learning experience. Because he was a man who had been chosen by God to be a man of wisdom and wealth. After going through the temptation of lust and having all richest in the world.

He surrendered himself too many women, and he failed so many times. After a while, he lost his desire to follow the faith of his father, David. We will be searching through this story for more encouragement that will benefit us in our way of life.

Solomon sought God:

Solomon was the son of King David. As we know, David reigned over the land of Israel for forty years. In fact, King Solomon reigned forty years as well. God appointed him to rule over

Israel to make peace with great wisdom around the region.

Solomon received an eagerness to seek God. He desired to experience the nature and the character of God. Even at an early age, he was hungry and thirsty for God.

Solomon was the only one of King David's sons to receive the honor of being anointed as the king of Israel.

David told him to build the temple for God, and he promised his father, King David. He would build a Jewish Temple in Jerusalem for the Lord.

Solomon Asked for Wisdom:

Solomon sought God, and He came to him in a dream and asked Solomon what his heart's desire was. God thought that he might ask for wealth and for help in conquering the enemy and maintaining his authority over other nations.

But Solomon answered and only asked to understand how to have the wisdom to rule over the people in order to promote justice.

God gave him wisdom, and besides that, He gave him wealth and allowed him to make peaceful relationships with the nations during his reign over Israel.

"behold, I have done according to your words; see, I have given you a wise and understanding heart, so that there has not been anyone like you before you, nor shall any like you arise after you." 1 Kings 3:12, NKJV.

Story of Two Women:

One of the greatest stories of King Solomon tells of how he performed an outstanding act of judgment. In this story, two women came before the king; they had a baby with them, but each woman claimed that the baby belonged to her.

They were asking King Solomon to bring justice to this situation. Solomon said, "Both of you are saying this baby is yours, and so I will be fair to both of you.

I will cut the baby in half. One of you will take half, and the other woman will take half of the baby with her."

The real mother said, *"No, do not kill the baby. I want her to have the baby. Let the baby live."* So, King Solomon discovered the birth mother was the one who was willing to give up the baby so that it would not be killed. They gave the baby to the birth mother.

"Then the woman whose son was living spoke to the king, for she yearned with compassion for her son; and she said, "O my lord, give her the living child, and by no means kill him!"

But the other said, "Let him be neither mine nor yours, but divide him." So the king answered and said, "Give the first woman the living child, and by no means kill him; she is his mother." 1 Kings 3:26-27, NKJV.

Solomon Committed Sins:

He completed many building projects, **"But Solomon took thirteen years to build his own house; so he finished all his house."** 1 Kings 7:1, NKJV.

Solomon also committed many sins in the sight of God. The Lord appeared to him twice and told him not to follow after other gods, but he had such lust and a strong sexual desire.

He pursued sexual pleasure with many foreign women, and he invited many queens and princesses into his palace. He had a lust relationship with many women, and these women turned his heart away from God.

In fact, the Bible says that Solomon had seven hundred wives and three hundred concubines. **"And he had seven hundred wives, princesses, and three hundred concubines; and his wives turned away his heart."** 1 Kings 11:3, NKJV.

God saw this, and He was angry with Solomon, **"So the Lord became angry with Solomon, because his heart had turned from the Lord God of Israel, who had appeared to him twice,"** 1 King 11:9, NKJV.

God did not take away his kingdom because of David's sake, but He said, *"I will bring adversaries into your kingdom."* Solomon's son Rehoboam rebelled against his father, Solomon, causing a division of the kingdom, but Rehoboam became the king of Israel.

Disobedience brings Judgments:

When we disobey God, our hearts can become cold through money, power, and the lust of the world. It will fill our hearts with a false desire for the material things of the world.

The Bible says that in the last day's people will have a cold heart toward God. They will love themselves more than they love God.

Our obedience brings blessing to us; disobedience will bring judgments. Let's be encouraged as we learn through the life of Solomon.

1. Solomon sought the Lord, how to search to know and to obey God. When we seek Him with our hearts, we shall find Him.

2. When we really honor our God, He is able to honor us.

3. He is calling us to His Kingdom, and He qualifies us to accomplish a task. We must rely on Him.

4. We must remind ourselves that He is the One who establishes the task. He is the One also who will complete the task through us.

5. We should desire to ask God to fill us with an enthusiastic heart to finish the task, not disobey His assignment.

Solomon Wrote Books:

In this kind of story, we read and understand that God anointed Solomon to bring justice to the nation through his wisdom. It encourages us through these stories that God knows our hearts, and He knows our situation.

He is a great judge, and He will bring justice to our situation. He is the One who will resolve our problems; He is the problem solver. Solomon created knowledgeable writings in the form of many proverbs and songs.

"He spoke three thousand proverbs, and his songs were one thousand and five." 1 Kings 4:32, NKJV.

Discernment for the Right People:

We seek God to give us discernment of the spirit to recognize the right people. We must ask Him to remove the wrong people out of our lives and bring the right people into our future.

We must remember that living outside of God is becoming meaningless. Living with the will of God to be pleasing on the Lord. No matter what we have done or achieved in life.

Seeking God must be first in our lives, more than anything else in life. If we remain faithful, He will pour down the mighty blessing of God over us. Amen.

The Story of Ezra

THE FULL STORY OF Ezra is about rebuilding the Temple of Solomon after Ezra came back from exile to Jerusalem. He had the ambition to return from Babylonian captivity and restore the religion and government back to Israel.

As we learn, Ezra was a priest and a scribe. He had the brilliant purpose of bringing the worship of the Lord God of Israel back to the Jewish people based on the Law of Moses.

The people had discovered that they desired to come back to build up their land and strengthen their faith according to their forefathers. They believed that the second hero and the great leader Ezra had come back after Moses.

They identified that God had fulfilled His promise to rebuild their land again after seventy years of captivity.

Ezra Needed Hearing God:

Ezra had a fear of God, and he loved to learn about the God of Israel. What a fantastic desire he had to pursue and search for God. His passion for serving the will of God.

In his time, he was in need to hear God for direction to lead the people who had been in captivity for many years.

"For Ezra had prepared his heart to seek the Law of the Lord, and to do it, and to teach statutes and ordinances in Israel." Ezra 7:10, NKJV.

Restore Their Faith:

People were ready for transformation in their land and to restore their religious inheritance back in their hearts. Ezra was studying and practicing the Law of the Lord.

He chose to prepare himself to move to the next level of understanding and worship the God of Israel. He had a passion for growing up more to teach the Law of the Lord.

So that although they were not able to learn and to worship God before in Babylon. Now they could worship God in their own land.

It requires preparation to establish a strong task for the Kingdom of God. The way Ezra completed gives us a fantastic way to look at his background.

He was far away from the Temple of God. He was looking forward to being free to study more about God and worship Him through the Law of the Lord.

Completed the Temple:

In this story of Ezra, he knew this was the right thing to do in his time. We can see that Ezra had the heart to rebuild the Temple of God. Ezra arrived to rebuild the Temple so that there would be a place of worship.

There will time for the people to dedicate themselves to God. He appeared to rebuild it to lead to triumph and victory, but God was involved in this project of restoration.

Of course, it wasn't easy, to begin with, administering, and providing all the blueprint construction. There were all the materials needed, but God was in charge. He is always the provider for His House.

He finished after twenty years, and he was able to bring the people of God together to worship again. God is still in control of all situations, and He will bring an end to restore what was lost.

Encouraging Word:

The encouraging word here is that no matter how many years people were under the regime of darkness or any other evil captivity. Now in the New Covenant, we are under Grace.

We are the Temple of God. The Holy Spirit lives in us. The moment we acknowledge Jesus as the Son of God and accept Him as our Savior. We repent our sins, and we invite Him into our hearts. Then, we are saved by His Grace.

We believe our name is written in the book of life in Heaven. He is dwelling in our spirit and soul. We worship Jesus in spirit and truth. Jesus died for our sins to bring us back to the relationship with the Father again. Amen.

The Story of Nehemiah

IN THE STORY OF Nehemiah, we understand that Ezra's rebuilding the Temple of God. He has completed a great accomplishment. The people returned to worship God and to live under the guidance of the Lord.

And yet there was no security for the city of Jerusalem. There was a lot of fear of a new attack by the surrounding enemies in the region. The city needed a wall to protect the people.

They would have preferred to have surrendered by a wall of stone to have security and stability from their enemies.

Nehemiah sent by the King:

Nehemiah was a man who was serving the king, and he had a high official position. He stayed with King Artaxerxes in the capital city of Susa.

"O Lord, I pray, please let Your ear be attentive to the prayer of Your servant, and to the prayer of Your servants who desire to fear Your name; and let Your servant prosper this day, I pray, and grant him mercy in the sight of this man. For I was the king's cupbearer." Nehemiah 1:11, NKJV.

He became the cupbearer for the king, and he had found favor in the king's heart. He requested that the king allow him to go back to Jerusalem as the governor of the people in order to build the wall to surround the city.

He took the chance to obey the call of God, and he prayed that he would have favor in the king's heart.

Nehemiah had a good life in this position of serving the King. He knew that there were more blessings out there if he continued to be a part of God's plan. The king granted his request.

"And I said to the king, "If it pleases the king, and if your servant has found favor in your sight, I ask that you send me to Judah, to the city of my fathers' tombs, that I may rebuild it." Nehemiah 2:5, NKJV.

God Prepared Everything:

We recognize here that God had arranged all of these projects and ideas in Nehemiah's heart. He felt that there was no protection in Jerusalem, that there was nothing to surround the city.

Nehemiah had a strong faith and belief that God would make way for him to restore the wall around Jerusalem.

He couldn't do anything on his own. When he couldn't function in his service in the presence of King Artaxerxes of Persia. Even the king noticed that there was something wrong in Nehemiah's face.

When we have something in our hearts, we cannot hide it; everyone can see it. And most importantly, our Father in heaven sees everything that is going on in our thoughts.

We may sometimes feel like giving up our faith and not trusting God. When there seems to be no protection from God surrounding our lives. But when we experience God with us, who can be against us.

"What then shall we say to these things? If God is for us, who can be against us?" Romans 8:31, NKJV.

God Used Nehemiah:

God could have used anybody during that time of Nehemiah. But God had Nehemiah in His mind to use him in a unique location and at a specific time.

God sent Nehemiah to lead this project for a short time. He could not be afraid of intimidation from any nation around the region.

Are we hearing God's voice and understanding God's plan in order to obey His will?

It is our faith operating in the realm of the Spirit of God that will place the shield of protection over our lives. The Bible said:

"No weapon formed against you shall prosper, And every tongue which rises against you in judgment

You shall condemn. This is the heritage of the servants of the Lord, And their righteousness is from Me, Says the Lord." Isaiah 54:17, NKJV.

Completed the Wall:

The city of Jerusalem is very historical and is important to God. Where God will have His City and the place where God would dwell in His house. And yet there was still no protection around the city.

Because the enemy could have been attacking them at any moment in the city, destroying everything. They have fixed it from the past. But the Wall was not strong enough for the people, and they were in danger of being attack again.

And so, the people had a passion for rebuilding a strong wall of stone in order to protect the city and the people.

God saw that the wall was a significant and important project to be built as soon as possible. Under the leadership of Nehemiah, they built the wall around the city of Jerusalem within fifty-two days.

"So the wall was finished on the twenty-fifth day of Elul, in fifty-two days." Nehemiah 6:15, NKJV.

Encouraging Word:

The story of passion and dedication will encourage us because the city needed the wall for safety. It would have been like a house with no outside wall of security. There would continually make fear and worries of an enemy attack.

In the same way, the faith in Christ that we have inside our hearts will give us confidence that we are in the Lord Jesus. But we also need protection so that we will not get attacked outside of our lives by the enemy.

The protection of our faith is the Word of God. We decree the blood of the Lamb of God over every area of our homes, churches, jobs, and families. Amen.

The Story of Esther

THE STORY OF ESTHER tells us about a brave woman who came from a Jewish family. Her name would remain in the Bible and would be recorded throughout history.

Studying the book of Esther, we cannot find any word "God" or "Lord." She didn't know that Almighty God would take her through a phenomenal challenge of her life.

The Lord has organized the right place that would lead her into the palace of King Ahasuerus.

And our Christian life even today remembers this strong woman who would inspire us through the centuries.

As born-again Christians, we all can rejoice that God is able to turn every hardship experience into a new life. We celebrate the freedom we now have in Christ. God was at work throughout this entire story.

Events for the King:

King Ahasuerus had an enormous Persian empire. His kingdom consisted of 127 provinces and was filled with power and wealth.

In most of the events of the day, the king needed to enjoy and demonstrate his power in public. So, the king asked his queen, Vashti, to appear for him and his guests with her beauty on display, wearing a crown in a public event.

"to bring Queen Vashti before the king, wearing her royal crown, in order to show her beauty to the people and the officials, for she was beautiful to behold." Esther 1:10, NKJV.

On the day of the event, Queen Vashti refused to appear in front of the public. The king became furious, and he ordered that Queen Vashti may not be allowed to ever return in the king's presence.

They banished Queen Vashti. Then, it was announced that they would have to search throughout the land for a beautiful new virgin queen for the king.

Esther Chosen as a Queen:

They brought in many girls, and ultimately Esther was chosen as a candidate for the king in his palace.

Esther lived in the citadel of Susa. She lost her parents and have passed away, and her uncle Mordecai had adopted her as his own daughter.

Mordecai had a position in service in an official area of the king's palace. He knew that it needed a new queen for the king.

"So it was, when the king's command and decree were heard, and when many young women were gathered at Shushan the citadel, under the custody of Hegai, that Esther also was taken to the king's palace, into the care of Hegai the custodian of the women." Esther 2:8, NKJV.

The Bible mentions that the king loved Esther more than all the other girls who came to meet the king. The King chose Esther out of all other girls alone.

So, Esther had the favor of God and was chosen by the king to become his queen. Mordecai reminded her not to identify herself or reveal her Jewish identity as she came from a Jewish background.

"The king loved Esther more than all the other women, and she obtained grace and favor in his sight more than all the virgins; so he set the royal crown upon her head and made her queen instead of Vashti." Esther 2:17, NKJV.

An Assassination Plot:

Later on, Mordecai found out that there was an assassination plot in the palace against King Ahasuerus. He reported the details of the plot to Queen Esther. The king had also heard of the plot, and the king gave him attention.

Esther and Mordecai wanted to protect the king from his enemies. The king decided to appoint a man who would oversee his government affairs and rule over all of the top officials in the palace.

"In those days, while Mordecai sat within the king's gate, two of the king's eunuchs, Bigthan and Teresh, doorkeepers, became furious and sought to lay hands on King Ahasuerus." Esther 2:21, NKJV.

King Chosen Haman:

The man was named Haman, and he was a descendant of Agag, the king of the Amalekites. So, they have sworn the descendants of Agag were enemies of Israel for past generations. Even until the time of Haman.

He had such a dark-rooted and hateful heart toward the Jewish people. He eventually ordered that all the official members of the government kneel down at the king's gate to honor him. Except Mordecai would not do what he had ordered them to do.

"After these things King Ahasuerus promoted Haman, the son of Hammedatha the Agagite, and advanced him and set his seat above all the princes who were with him." Esther 3:1, NKJV.

Destruction of Jewish People:

When the royal officials discovered that Mordecai had not done. What they had ordered him to do, they told Haman that Mordecai was a Jew.

Haman made a plan to punish Mordecai, and also to wipe out all the Jewish people, destroying them in every region of the land.

"But he disdained to lay hands on Mordecai alone, for they had told him of the people of Mordecai. Instead, Haman sought to destroy all the Jews who were throughout the whole kingdom of Ahasuerus—the people of Mordecai." Esther 3:6, NKJV.

The time of the annihilation planned, when all the Jews, from adults to young children, were arriving. Esther discovered what was going on, and she sent a message to Mordecai.

He told Esther to ask the king for mercy and remove the decree, which should not be followed.

There was another law in place that no one could ever be allowed to enter the presence of the king. Suppose they had not first been invited. Esther had not been into the presence of the king for three days.

Mordecai appealed to her to go to the king. However, she can plead with him for the salvation of all the Jewish people.

Three Days Fasting:

Esther asked that all the Jewish people would fast for three days, and then she would go into the king. She said that she would go into him without an invitation.

"Go, gather all the Jews who are present in Shushan, and fast for me; neither eat nor drink for three days, night or day. My maids and I will fast likewise. And so I will go to the king, which is against the law; and if I perish, I perish!" Esther 4:16, NKJV.

After three days, she kept her word and went into the palace, risking her own life for her people. But the moment the king saw her, he was pleased with Esther.

He reached out his hands with the gold scepter to accept her presence. Esther then invited both the king and Haman back to her palace for a banquet, and the king accepted her invitation.

"If I have found favor in the sight of the king, and if it pleases the king to grant my petition and fulfill my request, then let the king and Haman come to the banquet which I will prepare for them, and tomorrow I will do as the king has said." Esther 5:8, NKJV.

King Honored Mordecai:

The king asked Haman. "What shall be done unto the man whom the king delighted to honor?"

Haman thought that the king was planning to honor him, but the king had another man in mind—and that man was Mordecai. He ordered Haman to honor Mordecai by taking him into the city.

"So Haman came in, and the king asked him, "What shall be done for the man whom the king delights to honor?" Now Haman thought in his heart, "Whom would the king delight to honor more than me?" Esther 6:6, NKJV.

Haman did what the king told him to do, which was to parade Mordecai around the city. Allow him to wear a royal robe and set him upon a horse. He was leading him through the city to honor the man whom the king delighted to honor.

"Then let this robe and horse be delivered to the hand of one of the king's most noble princes, that he may array the man whom the king delights to honor. Then parade him on horseback through the city square, and proclaim

before him: 'Thus shall it be done to the man whom the king delights to honor!'" Esther 6:9, NKJV.

Haman Built a Gallow:

Haman had an evil spirit within him and leading him to demolish and destroy God's chosen people. Haman's family and his wife and friends all suggested that he should destroy the Jewish people. They gave Haman the idea to build up gallows on which to hang Mordecai.

"Then his wife Zeresh and all his friends said to him, "Let a gallows be made, fifty cubits high, and in the morning suggest to the king that Mordecai be hanged on it; then go merrily with the king to the banquet. And the thing pleased Haman; so he had the gallows made." Esther 5:16, NKJV.

Haman even went to the king to ask permission to hang Mordecai upon the gallows, but the favor of God was upon Mordecai.

Banquet for the King and Haman:

The first day Esther served the meal, but then she invited the king and Haman back tomorrow for yet another banquet.

Esther noticed that on the second day of her planned feasts. God was making a change in her people's lives in a supernatural way.

She wanted to save the entire Jewish nation. She knew justice must speak up that the devil is a liar, and he must be defeated.

"So Esther answered, "If it pleases the king, let the king and Haman come today to the banquet that I have prepared for him." Esther 5:4, NKJV.

The Second day of Banquet:

On the second day, when the king and Haman went to Esther's banquet, the king was again pleased with Esther. He asked her, *"What is your petition?"*

"the second day, at the banquet of wine, the king again said to Esther, "What is your petition, Queen Esther? It shall be granted you. And what is your request, up to half the kingdom? It shall be done!" Esther 7:1-2, NKJV.

Esther speaks up with her desire and passion for the Jewish people. She had such courage and a great determination to stand up for justice. She had to confront the situation with the king. She spoke with the spirit of boldness.

"For we have been sold, my people and I, to be destroyed, to be killed, and to be annihilated. Had we been sold as male and female slaves, I would have held my tongue, although the enemy could never compensate for the king's loss." Esther 7:4, NKJV.

The king asked who that man was, and who would dare to do such things? Esther answered that he is right here with us that the man is Haman.

This enraged the king so greatly that he left to go to the garden palace. While he was gone, Haman began to beg Esther for his life. He drew very close to her bed, pleading for mercy from Esther.

At that very moment, the king came back into the room. He saw Haman close to the queen's bed and thought that Haman was trying to molest Esther.

King Ordered Hang Haman:

The king ordered that Haman would be hanged on the very gallows he had built for Mordecai. Haman had thought that he would build the gallows for someone else and not for himself.

The heart of Haman was evil and full of darkness, filled with the hateful desire to destroy other people. He tried and sought to destroy the Israelites.

"So they hanged Haman on the gallows that he had prepared for Mordecai. Then the king's wrath subsided." Esther 7:8, NKJV.

As we study the book of Esther that the people of God will always prevail over an evil man named Haman. Through this, we learn that everything happens for a reason. Haman thought that no one could read his mind.

We would do well to remember the law of sowing and reaping, that everything comes from the heart. When God looks down and hears the cries of His people, He will do a supernatural miracle for us all.

King Promoted Mordecai:

After the death of Haman, they gave his estate to Mordecai. It's also offered him all the government authority that Haman had before. They gave Mordecai the seal and the king's signet ring.

The king established a new decree that would be written, a new law for the Jews. It would allow them the right to defend themselves from any future attack, as well as to keep their own language.

They spread the great news of victory throughout all the provinces. They celebrated and rejoiced as free Jewish people. God made victory for them to have a new life of prosperity.

Encouraging Word:

The encouraging word here is the magnificent way that God in this story watched over His people, Israel. He fulfilled His promise to surround them with the hand of His care and love.

The enemy cannot have God's people, even though he has tried to wipe out the Jews from all the provinces. God sees the hearts and hearing the prayers of His people, and He used one young woman to change the course of Jewish history.

The Jews could have perished, but God got involved in the situation, and He saved them all. Praise His name, and glory be to God forever.

Today, in Israel, the entire Jewish nation and they still celebrate the **Feast of Purim** as a Jewish holiday. It reminds them of the God of Israel who rescued them from destruction.

The Story of Job

IN THIS STORY, WE will study the life of a man who had a *"faith under trial"* experience turned back to live again. The man had the faith to grasp how to trust God. He is pleased when His people trust Him.

We must understand how to have a fear of God. God is waiting for us to give us victory. We build up our faith by the Word and to trust in our Lord Jesus. At the same time, we live in challenging circumstances.

Job was the man who had everything, including a good heart with the fear of the Lord. God was pleased with him, and he chose to be obedient. He devoted himself to God, and he was well known as a man of integrity, as well as a wealthy man.

Lucifer Exult Himself:

In this situation, God set up a meeting with one of the angel Lucifer, also called Satan. He wanted to have all authority and control. The

Bible mentions two other angels: Michael, Gabriel.

As we know, all angels were created by God to serve and to take a message from God to chosen people.

Satan was the worship leader in heaven, but he wanted to be worshiped and to become like God. The Word tells us that Satan said to himself.

"I will make myself like the Most High." So, God cast him out from heaven down to earth. "I will ascend above the heights of the clouds, I will be like the Most High." Isaiah 14:14, NKJV.

God Talks with Satan:

God asked Satan and what he answered God: *"From roaming throughout the earth, going back and forth on it."*

"And the Lord said to Satan, "From where do you come?" So Satan answered the Lord and said, "From going to and fro on the earth, and from walking back and forth on it." Job 1:7, NKJV.

In this case, Satan appeared in the presence of God to seek permission to attack and destroy Job.

At the same time, God had blessed Job in everything, but God still allowed Satan to attack Job. But at the end of the conversation between God and Satan. Let's read this verse:

"But now, stretch out Your hand and touch all that he has, and he will surely curse You to Your face!" And the Lord said to Satan, "Behold, all that he has is in your power; only do not lay a hand on his person." So Satan went out from the presence of the Lord." Job 1:11-12, NKJV.

Bad Reports Arrived:

This story is given to help us understand the way of God's power to restore in times of destruction. Further, we must understand the nature of Satan, who was not allowed by God to touch Job. He could do nothing without God's permission.

Let's take a look at Job's life and learn about his family. He had a wife, seven sons, and three daughters, and he was the richest man in all the surrounding regions.

And yet, the Bible tells us that in one day, four messengers arrived at Job's house to give him different bad reports. Ultimately, he learned that he had just lost everything.

Four Messengers:

The first messenger arrived, saying, "when the Sabeans raided them and took them away—indeed they have killed the servants with the edge of the sword, and I alone have escaped to tell you!" Job 1:15, NKJV.

The second messenger arrived, saying, "While he was still speaking, another also came and said, "The fire of God fell from heaven and burned up the sheep and the servants, and consumed them, and I alone have escaped to tell you!" Job 1:16, NKJV.

The third messenger arrived, saying, "While he was still speaking, another also came and said, "The Chaldeans formed three bands, raided the camels and took them away, yes, and killed the servants with the edge of the sword; and I alone have escaped to tell you!" Job 1:17, NKJV.

The fourth messenger arrived, saying, "While he was still speaking, another also came and said, "Your sons and daughters were eating and drinking wine in their oldest brother's house, and suddenly a great wind came from across the wilderness and struck the four corners of the house, and it fell on the young people, and they are dead; and I alone have escaped to tell you!" Job 1:18-19, NKJV.

Job Worshiped God:

The Bible tells us that Job got up and tore up his robe, shaved his head, and fell on the ground to worship the Lord God.

"Then Job arose, tore his robe, and shaved his head; and he fell to the ground and worshiped." Job 1:20, NKJV.

The question came in his mind: why do bad things happen to good people? He lost his family, wealth, and health. He didn't blame God and even didn't curse God.

He just humbled himself to worship God. He learned that everything that had happened was completely out of his control. He couldn't do anything to stop the tragedies. He did not get angry, and he did not sin against God.

Job spoken with Friends:

In this tragedy, Job had three friends—Eliphaz, Bildad, and Zophar. They appeared to comfort him after all of these events took place. They tried to convince Job that all the suffering and catastrophes happened as punishment because of sins in his life.

But Job had another friend, Elihu, who told Job that he desired to become humble. He needed to submit to these trials of faith in order to purify himself to God.

According to the story, Job had such a wonderful character and a strong fear of God in his heart.

Regardless of his friends' advice, he still sought to purify himself and surrender everything unto God. This reveals to us that we must give ourselves over into God's hand. He is the One who knows every hardship and trouble that will ever come against us.

When we look back on our lives, we see that He is still the One who has delivered us from all adversaries for His glory.

Relationship with God "better:"

When Job heard of all the disasters that had calamities on him. He didn't understand why God had allowed these tragedies to strike him. It was a wake-up call on his life, reminding him to pursue God with his whole heart.

Let's concentrate on this outstanding word ***"better"*** to encourage us to stand strong even when a catastrophe is heading toward us.

• Job could recognize God *"better,"*

• Job could acknowledge God *"better,"*

• Job opened his spiritual eyes *"better,"*

• Job got a closer relationship with God *"better,"*

• Job learned how to trust God *"better,"*

• Job got more love for God *"better,"*

• Job grew into a humble man in the presence of God *"better."*

Job Asked three Questions:

In the meantime, Job had a hard time with what was going on in his family. His wife was not trying to comfort him and give him an encouraging word. She was criticizing him instead to refresh him.

"Then his wife said to him, "Do you still hold fast to your integrity? Curse God and die!" Job 2:9, NKJV.

What kind of comfort and encouragement did Job receive from his own family! Job asked several questions from God:

The **first** question was, **"Who can bring a clean thing out of an unclean? No one!"** Job 14:4, NKJV.

The **second** comment was, **"But man dies and is laid away; Indeed he breathes his last, And where is he?"** Job 14:10, NKJV.

The **third** question was, **"If a man dies, shall he live again? All the days of my hard service I will wait, Till my change comes."** Job 14:14, NKJV.

At the end of Job's story, we learn that God blessed him double to his health, wealth, and family. God brought back his happiness and gave him prosperity beyond what he had before.

What God makes a man higher than anything else? Nothing can comprehend the ways of God. He keeps all glory to Himself. Glory to His holy name!

Encouraging words:

We can study from this tragedy as we study no matter what situation takes place against us.

I can answer this question: Yes, we die, and yet we will live again in Christ. This is a wonderful promise that is found in the Word of God.

When we turn over our hearts and our lives to Him. We lay down our problems in the presence of God. We invite Jesus into our lives. He is walking with us.

When the enemy attacks us, we must be courageous to grow in God. We have the confidence of eternal life through His death and resurrection. We move forward to worship Him and honor Him. We must stay close to Him; He is the source for all the answers.

Even though we may not understand why righteous people frequently suffer in this life.

We don't have all the answers, but we can only trust God with what we experience, and the answers will come afterward.

If we continue to have a perfect relationship with the Lord. If we keep a humble attitude, we will have confidence that He has everything under control. We must trust Him; He is the One whom we love and adore. Amen.

The Book of Psalms

THESE INSPIRING MESSAGES PREPARE us as we read deeper into this book. The way King David worshiped God, and he provides us with an awesome practice. So that we can learn about worship, and it takes us into the spirit of worship and praise.

Most praise and worship music has been written through the book of Psalms. The book of Psalms is a magnificent collection of poetry.

It contains the fascinating experiences of worship, praise, and prayer that can lift us up into the heart of God.

The book is full of the Spirit of God, which directs us how to praise and worship God with a grateful heart. It divides the psalms and hymns into five books, expressions of praise to God.

Psalm Guides us to Worship:

Let's focus on the chapters for which the writer is David—from chapters 1 through 150. We learn these themes through the story of the book of Psalms.

God requires us to recognize who are our godly friends and who are our ungodly companion.

"Blessed is the man
Who walks not in the counsel of the ungodly,
Nor stands in the path of sinners,
Nor sits in the seat of the scornful;
But his delight is in the law of the Lord,
And in His law he meditates day and night."

Psalm 1:1-2, NKJV.

The psalms tell us that when God's people are in trouble, they lack God's guidance. We must have faith and trust in God, praying all the time.

The Lord God is the King; He is our judge, and He is our refuge, our protection. As we study and meditate on the book of Psalms. We learn that God was merciful to Israel despite their rebellion against God.

The book shows us how we should pray for the restoration of Israel and the peace of Jerusalem. God's covenant with Israel is established. When we look at the Word and read the Psalms, we see that He is a forgiving God.

David inspires us to praise the God of Israel. He explains how to experience God's grace and goodness and to obtain the salvation of the Lord.

Hallelujah and Praise:

We see through the book of Psalms that God's faithful love for His people is perfect and never-ending. David is proving that we must have a thankful heart and a lifestyle of gratitude.

Let's get ready to bring glory and honor to the name of the God of Israel. The word "Hallelujah" that is used in music is found in the book of Psalms. We as Christians are singing and saying, *"Praise the Lord, praise be unto the Lord Jesus."*

"Let everything that has breath praise the Lord. Praise the Lord!" Psalm 150:6, NKJV.

Your Marvelous Works:

We look at a great and awesome experience of His love. In fact, He answers our prayers, and that He is taking care of our lives.

We shall testify to everyone all of His marvelous performances. We cannot be silent because

He is good and because His mercy endures forever. Our spirits will witness that He is moving in our lives and directing our paths into a fantastic future.

He knows where our destiny leads, and so we will have no fear in our hearts. He has done extraordinary accomplishments every day. We cannot hold back and not tell of all His glory and miracles to those who need to hear about Him.

He is a perfect Father and takes care of His children. Trust in Him; He will not let you down. Never allow any doubt to grow in your heart; continue believing in Him.

"I will praise You, O Lord, with my whole heart; I will tell of all Your marvelous works." Psalm 9:1, NKJV.

"The Lord is my Shepherd":

We love Psalm 23, and we pick up a lot of inspiring words from this verse: **"The Lord is my Shepherd."**

You probably have heard many messages in the church about this verse. We must realize that Jesus is our Shepherd, that He is the One who looks over His sheep. We are His sheep, and He watches over us.

He is taking care of us in every small and serious obstacle of life. Jesus laid down His life for His sheep, and we may hear His voice. We receive protection and experience the love of God.

I believe King David had a passionate experience with God in an intimate way. He expressed himself to these realities, allowed him to praise and worship God in the Psalms.

"The Lord is my shepherd; I shall not want." Psalm 23:1, NKJV.

"Create in me a clean heart, O God":

When David fell into adultery with Bathsheba, and the prophet confronted him. David realized that God had seen everything.

He had thought he could hide all of his sins. David also thought he could cover every sin he had committed in his life.

So, he cried out from his heart to God for forgiveness, and he repented of his sins. God restored his life and brought him into a new season of blessings.

That's why he said in this verse: *"Create in me a clean heart, O God, create a right spirit in me."* Have we asked God to create a right spirit within us?

Yes, I have sought Him many times to create an excellent spirit in me, that my life would never disgrace His name.

"Create in me a clean heart, O God, And renew a steadfast spirit within me." Psalm 51:10, NKJV.

"With long life will I satisfy him":

This verse is my favorite passage in the book of Psalms because of the phrase *"with long life."* We know that the Lord came to the earth to save us and give us everlasting life.

That was the plan of the Father to send His only begotten Son to be born on this earth. He dies for our sins so that we can experience everlasting salvation.

Jesus shed His own blood to cleanse us from all our unrighteousness and to heal us from all our diseases. Here it is said, *"Show him my salvation."*

There will not be salvation for us if there is no death on the cross and no resurrection. Only by His death and resurrection do we have salvation, long and healthy life in our bodies.

When I minister to those who are sick in their bodies, I pray for healing. I speak life with a prosperous soul. I claim a long and healthy life to satisfy us on earth.

As we know, this is the grace of God has been released from heaven upon us. Because of the love of the Father, who loves us very much.

"With long life I will satisfy him, And show him My salvation." Psalm 91:16, NKJV.

"I will lift up my eyes to the hills":

This powerful verse encourages us to look up toward the Lord Jesus, and when we seek Him, we find Him.

This verse says, *"I will lift up my eyes to the hills."* This means that the Lord is always on high, and His throne is on a high over the earth. He is not down; He is higher than everything else.

When we look down on ourselves when we are lost, we cannot find Him. When we are focusing on our problems and concentrating on our own power. We lose every perfect blessing we have as a child of God.

We get down in our own selves, then the devil lying to us, and we lose our focus on Jesus. We become blind in our spiritual eyes.

We don't have any joy and peace in ourselves, and we have no peace with God. We get depressed, and we feel very down.

"I will lift up my eyes to the hills—From whence comes my help? My help comes from the Lord, Who made heaven and earth." Psalm 121:1-2, NKJV.

The verse goes on to say, *"My help comes from the Lord."* Have you ever sought the Lord?

Have you ever said, *"I need help, Lord! I need You to help me, Lord!"* Yes, I have sought many times for Him to restore me; without Him, I cannot survive.

I would even say that I cannot breathe without Your presence. I need Him all the time. I believe that David was saying to God, *"I need You, God; I know my help comes from You, Lord."*

David had enormous confidence in his heart. We can also speak this word that our help comes from the Lord.

This is a dynamic statement of faith, to believe that He is the only One on whom we must rely. Because no one else can save us as Jesus can. Let's say out loud: *"I believe in Jesus; my help, my joy, and my peace come from Jesus only."* Praise His Holy Name.

"I have sought your face with all my heart":

David was humbling himself to seek the Lord. He knew that pursuing God was not a waste of time. The more searching for God that we do, the better we will recognize and become strong in His presence.

Following the Lord will become easier when we are ready to lie down all of our lives at the feet of Jesus. As for myself, I lay down all my thoughts and my burdens about my future on the altar.

Every heart of a born-again Christian should be willing to seek Jesus to receive more of Him. He is there to release His fresh anointing on us. I leave my troubles there for Him at His feet.

The next line says, *"According to your promise,"* and we must remember that His promise is always there, for eternity. His words are truth and full of life. If we expect and trust in His promise, He will never ever let us down.

Seeking God should be enjoyable for us because His Spirit brings peace and joy to our souls. We need Him every day of our lives.

If we seek His face every day, we will not regret it. We will become even more mature, and we will experience more victories in the time of trouble day by day. Amen.

"I entreated Your favor with my whole heart; Be merciful to me according to Your word." Psalm 119:58, NKJV.

"Let everything that has breath praise the Lord":

God loves our praise and worship; our worship goes up to heaven, and it allows us to minister to the Lord Jesus. It also brings our spirits up to a higher level of devotion to Him.

Jesus said, **"But seek first the kingdom of God and His righteousness, and all these things shall be added to you."** Matthew 6:33, NKJV.

We learn how to worship and give Him thanks in our souls. We love Him because He loves us first.

The Word says, **"Let everything that has breath praise the Lord."** We receive a new spirit called the Holy Spirit. He is dwelling in our new spirits to help us worship Him with freedom without judgment and condemnation in Christ.

"Let everything that has breath praise the Lord. Praise the Lord." Psalm 150:6, NKJV.

Praise Him:

We praise Him with the joy of the Lord.

We praise Him because He created everything by His Word.

We praise Him because He has created us in His own image.

We praise Him because He sent His Son, Jesus, to die for us.

We praise Him because He is a good Savior and Lord forever.

We praise Him because He never fails us.

We praise Him because He is the everlasting Father to us.

Let's allow the Holy Spirit stirs our heart into mighty praise and worship, wherever we are! We are ready to honor Him by lifting up our hands and praising Him with sounds and expressions to move into His anointed music.

He wishes us to have an excellent spirit and a humble attitude. We give Him thanks all day long. We expect a glorious and magnificent ministry to come forward as we serve Him. Amen.

Proverbs, Ecclesiastes, and Song of Songs

ACCORDING TO SOME BELIEFS, King Solomon began to write *the Song of Solomon* in his youth. The book of *Proverbs* when he was in his middle age.

He wrote the book of *Ecclesiastes* when he became old. These three books became a part of God's Holy Word to man.

He had such a powerful authority of wisdom from Almighty God. He could communicate himself with Godly advice that any man can understand it. Then we can study and apply all Words of knowledge to our everyday life.

Proverbs

The book of Proverbs gathered all the wisdom of God. It's truly provided both teaching and discipline in fear of the Lord. It's instructed us to live in a godly life.

The book of Proverbs has no actual relation to the ancient record of the Israelites. This wisdom demonstrates the natural thought and purpose of effective knowledge.

The fear of the Lord is the full action of honoring God. Fear of the Lord is the beginning of wisdom to lead us into a great knowledge of God.

The Jewish in Israel considered that wisdom could be taken place from one generation to the next. So, they accepted it to achieve their intentions to know God better.

It's like the book of Psalms, where there are different writers, depending on which part of the book we are reading. During Solomon's reign, the nations of Israel were greatly wealthy.

When people are living in a luxury lifestyle, they usually ignored God. They neglected the basic laws of spiritual living in favor of earthly pleasures.

Proverbs encourage people to recognize God and to live a way that is pleasing to God.

Proverbs is written with a short text in spiritual advice.

The Proverbs might be simply recognized in Jewish congregations and all churches today. The Word of wisdom will have divine characters in the text of Proverbs who were presented by the revelation of God.

The Spirit of God is established His Word of Wisdom to all individuals' believers in all nations.

The Contents of Proverbs:

There are *four parts* in the textbook of **Proverbs.**

Chapters 1 to 9 would explain the significance of wisdom.

Chapters 10 to 24 would teach the fundamentals of wisdom.

Chapters 25 to 29 consist of numerous general truths and a portion of advice by Solomon, which were gathered.

Chapters 30 and 31 are the statements of Agur and Lemuel.

Chapter 30, Agur's stating a general truth concerning his views on life. Rather than looking to his own wisdom, He looked to God's wisdom.

Chapter 31, King Lemuel is revealed as a writer in the last book of Proverbs.

As we know, the Word of God is true, and the ultimate author is the Holy Spirit.

There is no error can be found in His Holy Word. We study His divine plan to lead us to everlasting life in Christ.

Ecclesiastes

The author of this book is Solomon, and some would assume it was written later in his life. The book of Ecclesiastes confirms everything created in life with the reason for it. It allows the Word to explain:

"What profit has a man from all his labor, in which he toils under the sun?" Ecclesiastes 1:3, NKJV.

Solomon had the authority to see the creation of God that also men pursue pleasure. Solomon had good abundances of possessions, and thus he could reach everything he wished to achieve.

He also had enormous influence, and then he could act on everything carefully. He was the wisest man and was able to instruct on the human condition.

It attributed the book to Solomon so we would take every word. If we believe God inspired the Bible. We can accept this Word, for the book itself declares to be written by Solomon. He also sought to find the significance of life in pleasure.

Many people are experiencing a continue living their own way of life today. Solomon next struggled to find the interest of life in richness.

He was an extremely wealthy man in power. He performed to get brighter in wisdom. Many people invest their entire lives in accumulating wealth.

When they pass away, they must leave behind all their possessions to someone else. It is not wrongful to have richness if someone desires to use it only for the Kingdom of God rightfully.

But only if we are pursuing God and asking Him for wealth. God wants us to plant a seed on the ground, to reap the harvest of His riches for His glory.

The money can buy all the materials things, but it is not the reason God placed a man in this world. It will depress those who are obsessed with material objects in this life and eternity.

Song of Songs

The magnitude of the Song of Solomon is to offer love and comfort. God established the intimate relationship between one man and one woman together.

It is pure and acceptable when they are given each other sincerely care for one another as a husband and wife. God designed the sexual relationship between husband and wife's enjoyment.

God accepts the affection of a husband to his wife to describe the passion that as Christ is head of His church.

We will see the Song of Solomon is a collection of love poems setting up a document of poetry. These characters who are present in this poem are: "King Solomon" is the bridegroom, the "Shulamite" maid is his bride who emphasizes in the Song of Songs.

She is merely specified once by the name "Shulammite," Her true personality is unfamiliar. Why would you gaze on the Shulammite as on the dance of Mahanaim"?

As we read;

"Return, return, O Shulamite; Return, return, that we may look upon you!" Song of Solomon 6:13, NKJV.

We can learn two wonderful messages from the Song of Solomon.

• First, it advises us that being married to one person, *"one husband and one wife,"* is written in which the Bible teaches us. It was God's original purpose for marriage. It is even God's design for marriage today.

"Therefore a man shall leave his father and mother and be joined to his wife, and they shall become one flesh." Genesis 2:24, NKJV.

• Second, it shows that sensual affection is desirable in marriage. But it is a sinful act outside of a marriage relationship.

Advise to Marriages:

The Song of Solomon is an affirmation by God of matrimonial love. It's significant to honor the marriage with a romantic purpose.

It teaches us that God only permits us to have sexual satisfaction within marriage.

This will lead us to understand that God has created a sexual desire. The writing is rejecting to get involved in sexual relationships outside of marriage.

Surely, this book may consist of the Bible's best study of marriage. It would tell us to resist any sinful temptation outside of our marriage. He wants to be faithful to our spouses. Amen.

Major and Minor Prophets

THE SOVEREIGNTY OF GOD chose these Major Prophets to carry out a message on behalf of God to the nations. The Lord has used these men to hear the voice of God.

These major prophets' names are *Isaiah, Jeremiah, Lamentations, Ezekiel, and Daniel.* It represents five books in the Old Testament.

It refers to the messages that could be a warning, a judgment, and victory over the forthcoming situations.

It's declared; they are watchmen of the nation. They are messengers of God. They are prophets to prophesy the future or an event. God called these men to stand strong alongside the priests to serve their people.

Major Prophets

They delivered their message to people from God in which was accurate words of God. The

Lord wanted to send His plan to make sure that His people would hear Him.

They were declaring a prediction for an event. The result was hearing the Word of the Lord forwarded to them as a warning or as encouragements.

Their themes were inspiring and challenging. But it still turns to make as a signal for the future. The message of these prophets was calling people to:

- *Come back to God,*
- *Turn away from sins,*
- *No disobedience,*
- *Receiving final atonement through the Messiah,*
- *Experience God is in authority.*

These men served in several methods. Their voices pointed out the Mosaic Law; carried out their assignment of warning;

- *opposing sin,*
declaring repentance,
confidence of forgiveness,
- *predicted the approaching judgment,*
- *the forthcoming Messiah,*
- *watchman for the house of Israel,*
- *spiritual rejection of a religious,*

- *form of cult worship,*
- *practices of sacrifice in the region.*

Isaiah:

Isaiah's letter has been written under the inspiration of the Spirit of God. He declares an invitation to the nation of Judah to come back to give themselves to God. He described the events of the upcoming future.

In most chapters of the book, he expresses complete disapproval towards Judah. They were departing from God and called for repentance.

As Isaiah announces, the other message presents a promise and comfort. The assurances of the coming Messiah will take place.

As Isaiah described: He is in authority over His people.

His name is the Lord of hosts,
He is the Holy One of Israel.
He is the Lord God of Israel.
He is the Mighty One of Israel.

Isaiah is writing the primary declaration of God as being Yahweh. It acknowledges him as the strongest prophet.

They generally saw his determination to deal with situations in a dynamic way. So, after 60 years of ministry, he started gaining the approval of the people.

Jeremiah:

The main topic of the book of Jeremiah will be learning about two major subjects. God's authority of judgment and the promise of recovery through despair.

Jeremiah often used an analogy to deliver his messages, but it looked like no one preferred to pay attention to him. This prophet had complete dissolution and separation.

It called him the "weeping prophet" and the "cautious servant." Jeremiah experienced very resistance, but he continued devoted with respectful reverence to be faithful to God of Israel.

Therefore, Jeremiah went through like a defeat throughout the course of his 40 years of ministry. He was extremely weak and poor; they forced him into prison, and he lived an outrageous life.

Lamentations:

In the Book of Lamentations, each chapter is considered as a unit poem. The prophet, Jeremiah, was the author of the book. He recognizes that God used the Babylonians to bring out punishment on Jerusalem.

God had revealed to him for the forthcoming judgment. Because of their separation and the action of resisting authority.

They would go through the loss of Jerusalem! Jeremiah's reason for which the main object was to show the people what their refusal to obey the law of God.

If they did not turn their way back to God, they would have destruction. It's appealed to his writing of Lamentations, a funeral song for a people of God.

Jeremiah had a great passion for his nation. Lamentations make it evident that sin is an act of violence and releases God's wrath.

Expressing deep grief is acceptable in hard times, which ultimately turns into trusting God.

Ezekiel:

Ezekiel grew up in Jerusalem, and his name means "strengthened by God." He has served as a priest in the temple. While he was in Babylon. He became a prophet.

We see after the destruction of Jerusalem took place and Ezekiel's prophecies for the hope of the future.

Ezekiel came to himself to realize that he must prepare a proclamation of the faithfulness of God. He was declaring the hope of the Living King and a prophecy to ensure the redemption of his people.

We see Ezekiel freely accepted to surrender everything to God. He was further an early part of the hearing of the occupation and downfall of Jerusalem.

The Lord ordained Ezekiel to be a prophet but throughout his ministry. They forced him out to Babylon. He established an interest in others, looking after those unable to care for themselves.

He had a shepherd's heart with a strong burden for the priesthood, the place of worship for the glory of God.

When we are firmly refusing to obey the authority of God. He cannot bring us back to Himself unless we wake up, turn from our own ways, and acknowledge Him.

Daniel:

The book of Daniel is fascinating. It focuses on God's mighty supremacy and the unique fulfillment of God's plan. The Lord has special favor and protection upon Daniel and his friends.

Daniel had an extraordinary gift that God has given him to interpret dreams and visions for the coming millennium. They were in Babylonian captivity; these Hebrew's partners of Daniel had something in mind.

The Lord gave them a great capability to overcome the fear and special support of King Nebuchadnezzar. They granted Daniel and his colleagues serving positions in the Babylonian administration.

These dreams presented to give Daniel with a translation of the king's visions and powerful points of view of the forthcoming.

The book of Daniel is a guide to the Book of Revelation in the New Testament. It presents the prophecy of the sharing a defined nature of regimes and kingdoms of the world throughout history.

It will contribute in terms of what is being represented by each government. They have predicted it correctly.

Minor Prophets

God ordains these servants for their assignments to become Minor Prophets. Because of the importance of their prophetic messages to the nation. At the same effect, these Prophets had words to deliver to the people.

Mostly, God can use an ordinary person to deliver messages of God. However, their efforts were essential, not simply to individual peoples of the Northern or Southern Kingdoms of Israel at that season.

There are still powerful messages of God from Minor Prophets that can be studied throughout the generations, including now.

The Bible's Minor Prophets can be known from their books present: *Hosea, Joel, Amos, Obadiah, Jonah, Micah, Nahum, Habakkuk, Zephaniah, Haggai, Zechariah, Malachi.*

In summary of these messages include affirmations, promises, and predictions for disobedience to God. They also prepare for the coming of the Messiah in the New Covenant.

Hosea

The book of Hosea shows us a true manifestation of God's eagerness for mercy. He knew His eternal passion for those who seek Him. God instructed Hosea to marry the woman, Gomer.

He recognized that she would be a woman who commits adultery. So, Hosea obeyed God; he married her, and after they had three children.

Even though sometimes after Gomer became a mistress to another man. God ordered Hosea to take her back and to take care of her. The Lord wanted him also to forgive her.

Hosea's story represented God's interest to forgive Israel. It informs us how the people of God had turned into idol worship. We can see through this book that with the love of God, His compassion and recovery is available.

Joel

The book of Joel is a straightforward sign referring to God's judgment. His writing speaks of natural calamities and a ravaging plague. The reason of his prophecy is to claim the people to repentance and to encourage them.

And to inform those people who are looking for a comforter. It's a promise that the Holy Spirit would take place. We recognize the promise fulfilled in the book of Acts years later.

It was revealed we could be encouraged the comfort of the Holy Spirit is even possible to get today. Two notices in Joel described informing: God's judgment to irreligious, immoral nations. He will empower those who continue to be truthful and faithful.

Obadiah

The book of Obadiah is the briefest writing, as it is only 21 verses long. The prophet Obadiah gives this opportunity to express his disapproval of Edom for committing sins against God and Israel.

As we know, there were two descendants have been established by two twins' brothers.

The Edomites were descendants of Esau, and then the Israelites were descendants of Jacob.

A fall of these twins' brothers has changed relationships with each other between their descendants for over 1,000 years.

This conflict created the Edomites to prevent Israel from passing over their territory during the Israelites' Exodus from Egypt. Edom's sins now require a powerful message of judgment from God.

Obadiah's theme is decisive and strong, and the kingdom of Edom will be completely wiped out. Edom has been ineffective; they were rejoicing over Israel's tragedies.

When opposition force equipped for fighting on land invade Israel. The Israelites pleaded for support, but the Edomites reject to help and instead decide to fight against them.

The book finishes with the assurance of the accomplishment and salvation of Zion in the last days. When the nation will be brought back to God's people as He reigns over them.

Jonah

The book of Jonah is a record that speaks about how Jonah went from disobedient to obedient. Only then he was ready to serve the Lord. In fact, through some miraculous circumstances, God persuaded him to surrender himself to follow God's plan.

Jonah finally gave up himself to accept God's call to preach the Word. Jonah had a visitation from God, instructing him to proclaim the salvation of God to the nations of Nineveh and to encourage them to seek repentance.

Jonah was not very happy to hear God's call on him, as it was a very scary situation for him. Instead of obeying God and doing what He told him to do. He was running from God, not admitting the reality of God's desire to save the people of Nineveh.

The city was very close to where Jonah lived. He hides himself from God. He traveled to Joppa to get on a ship to the city of Tarshish located across the sea. His refusal to obey the authority of God has brought suffering upon himself.

Not Obeying God:

Jonah thought to stay away from God much better and not to proclaim the Word in the city. He decided to get on the ship to Tarshish, and there came a strong storm. The fellow workers on the ship called upon their gods to save them.

At the same time, Jonah was sleeping in the ship's bottom. So, these fellows found him as he was asleep. They woke him up and asked of him to pray to his God to save their lives from the storm.

Then the fellow's sailors cast lots to determine who had brought in suffering upon them. The lot went down on Jonah. He revealed himself as a Hebrew and trying to escape away from God.

Jonah finally convinced them that he was the one, and he told them who brought punishment from God. Jonah requested from the fellow's sailors to throw him into the sea.

Throw Him into Sea:

As instantly they tossed Jonah into the sea, the storm became calm. Rather than drowning, a big fish swallowed Jonah, and he was in the fish's belly for three days.

While Jonah was in the fish's belly, he cried out to acknowledge his failure and refusal to obey the authority of God. Then Jonah remembered that the Lord had instructed him to carry out the task.

Then God suddenly directed the fish to vomit him out to dry ground. Jonah was getting himself conscious of dry land. Jonah went to the city of Nineveh. He started to preach to the people; Jonah was not thrilled.

After his Preaching:

He went up to a mountain to see the Lord will wipe out the city. But God heard the people's repentance, He did not destroy, but He saved the whole city.

Jonah was not happy; at the same time, God was trying to teach Jonah a lesson. God created a gourd to grow (typically large fruit with hard skin). God wanted to protect Jonah from the sun. Awhile after that, God dried out the gourd, and Jonah got furious.

Eventually, God went on to show Jonah the irresponsibility of the event that he was worried about the gourd. He wants to remind him that the gourd had no life.

Then Jonah should better to be concerned in thousands of people who were going to everlasting suffering.

It is said angels sing and celebrate whenever a sinner turns from their evil ways and towards God. He loves His children; let's experience His love by asking Him to give us His mercy and blessings.

Micah

The book of Micah is a variety of messages about judgment and hope. One part, the Word has declared judgment upon Israel for people's sins, corrupt authority, and the worship of idols.

It hoped this judgment to end up in the process of being the damage of Samaria and Jerusalem. The passage shows not only the recovery of the nation. But the shift and an expression of extreme happiness of Israel and Jerusalem.

The prophet expresses complete disapproval of the rulers, priests, and prophets of Israel. Those who make full control of deceiving the people.

Because of their own efforts that Jerusalem will be wiped out. Micah commanded the rescued people leaving from Jerusalem to Babylon. It's finished with a warning for Jerusalem to break the nations who have made against her.

Micah declares the celebration of a remaining small part of Jacob. He calls for a time when God will remove the nation of idolatry and dependency by force.

God gives signs, so we will not have to face His extreme wrath. Our spiritual understanding of sins would help us make the right choice, so we would not reject His plan of blessings.

As a follower of Jesus, God will strengthen us because He loves us. We experience that sin will destroy every life. He wants us to become perfect in Him. This is the assurance of new life prepares to those who endure faithfully to Him.

Nahum

The theme of Nahum is comforting to Judah and to inform them the fall of Nineveh is the capital of Assyria. As we realize, Nineveh earlier had returned to God by hearing the preaching of Jonah.

Then 150 years later, the whole nations changed to their evil actions not to follow the Lord God. But Nineveh turned to the worship of idols, brutality, and pride.

God presents one of His prophets to Nineveh so that people can hear the prophecy about the judgment to make decisions for themselves.

Later again, He sends a message of repentance. But Nineveh's people could not decide to open their hearts to God. Nahum warned them, and God allowed the city to be brought under the authority of Babylon.

It horrifically describes Nahum's fiery statement of the cruel place. In the aftermath of their invasions by Babylon: they saw mounds of skulls, pierced bodies, imprisoned civilians, and extreme greed.

God is loving and patient. He waits for every nation to proclaim His name, and the people will accept Him as their Lord.

Any time a country turns its faith and people are separate themselves from Him to serve other gods. God acts with judgment. Let's pray that the Lord hears our prayer and heal our land.

Habakkuk

The prophet, Habakkuk, denounces the sins of Judah, is confronted with the event. God's chosen nations will have a bad experience with more enemies. Habakkuk's questions require him to rebuild trust in God's power, supremacy, and redemption.

Habakkuk is trying to tell his grief to God for getting an answer. Why the people of God can go through in their bondage.

"O Lord, how long shall I cry, And You will not hear? Even cry out to You, "Violence!" And You will not save." Habakkuk 1:2, NKJV.

God responds to him again and shows him a further message. Then Habakkuk addresses a petition revealing his steadfast confidence in

God, surely through these struggles. The Lord shows His answer to Habakkuk.

"Look among the nations and watch—Be utterly astounded! For I will work a work in your days, which you would not believe, though it were told you." Habakkuk 1:5, NKJV.

The Book of Habakkuk declares that God is a supreme ruler. He is an omnipotent God who has unlimited power. He has everything under His authority; He is able to do anything.

We just love to be silent in His presence and experience His Glory. The Lord Jesus is a life-changing miracle. He keeps His words and punishes evil; Jesus is sitting on the throne forever.

Zephaniah

It is recorded the writings of Zephaniah, during the rule of King Josiah, that he was a prophet to the people. Zephaniah's word of judgment and comfort consists of three main concepts:

God is a supreme ruler over all people.

Evil will bring about its own destruction, and God will defend the just.

God brings divine favor to those who express sincere regret and faith in Him.

Zephaniah speaks of the Lord's divine punishment on the entire earth, on Judah, on the neighboring nations, and Jerusalem. It's reflected by the actions of the Lord's grace on all people in Judah.

He is empowering us to move forward. He is lifting us to the highest calling to serve. We are created to be a part of His kingdom in this world.

Constantly, if we follow God's plan and His direction, then it becomes easy to live in His blessings. We may grow strong in faith and knowing Him through His Words.

As we experience, there is enough misery and hardship in the world. But if we lay down our heavy burned on the altar for Him.

We can trust in Him, we reach out to Him, and He will reach back into our lives from heaven with a great blessing. Amen.

Haggai

Haggai requested to ask for the people of God about their desires. He instructed them to respect and worship God by setting up the Temple despite resident and opposition activity.

Haggai ordered them not to be disheartened because they wanted to have a good temple. But this would not be entirely as good as Solomon's temple. He encouraged them to change their actions and to depend on God's absolute authority.

Haggai is an expression of the troubles the people of God dealt with this season. How the people enthusiastically established their trust in God. The Lord brought victory with more blessings to his nations.

Because the people of God set aside their desires and neglected to worship God in their hearts, it carried Judah into Babylonian exile.

The people of God chose their determination and needed to carry out based on God's words? God offered to tell the people to obey His words.

God informed them, but He further gave assurances through His servant Haggai to persuade them to accept Him.

As we look at Haggai points out with words of recovery and grace. God declares to worship, authority, and power over His people.

Zechariah

The Book of Zechariah will teach that salvation may all receive. Zechariah pointed out that God allows His prophets to be used to instruct, inform, and improve His people.

Sadly, they refused to accept the warning of God. Because of their sin would carry out God's discipline.

There is the last chapter that illustrates all nations of the world will enter into worship and honoring God. He wishes that all men seek Him. Zechariah declared that God is the supreme ruler over the earth.

His points of view for the ultimate manifestation that God looks at everything would take place. The characters of God's power are already showing in the world. He will carry out human actions to the conclusion.

It turns out to persuade them that it is not by the human's ability to pursue God, instead seek Him by the heart. He holds people accountable for their decisions in life. Zechariah's last point performs the force of natural reaction to God's authority.

Malachi

The Book of Malachi has prophetic predictions of the future. The message of the Lord to Israel to repent. The theme of Malachi was for the nations because God's preparing the people. However, God instructs the nations to change their heart to God.

God was delivering another mediator who would be between God, and man is the Messiah. They have expected for a long time. This is the last book of the twelfth of Minor Prophets, as the finished book of the Old Testament.

The proclamation of God's authority and the assurance of His recovery through the coming Messiah is a warning for the Israelites.

After four hundred years of expecting, it took place with fulfillment. It's finishing with an identical word from God's prophet, later John the Baptist, declaring;

"and saying, "Repent, for the kingdom of heaven is at hand!" Matthew 3:2, NKJV.

Because of God's love and His covenant with Israel, God has not forsaken His people. No matter, the people will not follow God's law and His commandment. But God still loves them, and His love is in our lives. Praise His name. Amen.

The New Covenant

THERE IS A PROMISE that God establishes with mankind. He makes an agreement that He will forgive sin. He will restore His relationship with those whose hearts are changed toward Him.

There is the mediator who is Jesus coming into the world by the Salvation of God to save humanity. Jesus' death on the cross is the evidence of His promise.

The New Covenant requires a complete transformation of heart, soul, spirit, and mind. It will take place so that God's people are easily gratifying onto Him.

It has also declared the message of the New Covenant.

"I will give you a new heart and put a new spirit within you; I will take the heart of stone out of your flesh and give you a heart of flesh.

I will put My Spirit within you and cause you to walk in My statutes, and you will keep My judgments and do them" Ezekiel 36:26-27, NKJV.

We recognize the Old Covenant that God had made with His people required obedience and submission with the Mosaic Law. I just want to mention the meaning of **Mosaic Law:** *"It's another term for the Law of Moses."*

The Law expected that the people observe regular sacrifices to be restored from their sins. Basically, the New Covenant was given to Israel to get saved.

God keeps an agreement to make them a fruitful nation, peaceful land with prosperity in the Promised Land. It was under the Old Covenant required; the Israelites to sacrifice animals as sin offerings to God.

When God commanded, this is an act of obedience to slay an animal as shedding the blood to cover their sins. But we are washed and cleansed by the blood of the Lamb of God.

God has committed to forgiving the sins of those who are in the new covenant. Therefore, new life in Christ has two main aspects: an inner part of spiritual renewal appearing in a fresh relationship with the Lord Jesus.

Then by inviting Jesus as Lord and Savior in our hearts with new faith, we are a new creation in Christ. When Jesus arrived to finish the plan of God.

He died on the cross, and He rose again from the dead. Therefore, we will no longer be under the Law. The Grace of God took place by Jesus, winning the victory.

The Old Covenant has given for which everything remained. Now we praise God that Jesus has taken over with a better covenant as King of Kings.

Now He is the Savior, which he is the advocate to the old one. Since He provides a new life to come and dwell in our spirit.

"But now He has obtained a more excellent ministry, inasmuch as He is also Mediator of a better covenant, which was established on better promises." Hebrews 8:6, NKJV.

John the Baptist:

The plan of God came with authority to John Baptist. He was willing to make way for what

Almighty God wanted to accomplish through him. As we know, Elizabeth, the mother of John and Mary, the mother of Jesus, was pregnant at the same time.

We know the angel of Lord Gabriel had already appeared to Zechariah about the supernatural birth and prophetic ministry of John. The Bible reveals John's birth from his mother, Elizabeth.

"And it happened, when Elizabeth heard the greeting of Mary, that the babe leaped in her womb; and Elizabeth was filled with the Holy Spirit." Luke 1:41, NKJV.

Two Mothers Met each other:

When the two mothers met, something pleasant and interesting happens. The baby, John, jumped within Elizabeth's womb as it filled her with the Holy Spirit.

The good news was a wonderful response to prayer because Elizabeth was barren and couldn't have a child.

John was growing into the spirit of God, who was chosen to be a messenger. The Lord sent him to prepare the way for the arrival of Jesus, the Messiah.

The significant authority is given to John to have the honor of baptizing Jesus in the Jordan River. John appeared with courage as he confronted even Herod, telling him that he must repent of his sins.

So, Herod had John the Baptist arrested and put him in prison. Later on, Herod beheaded John. Jesus declared about him.

"For I say to you, among those born of women there is not a greater prophet than John the Baptist; but he who is least in the kingdom of God is greater than he." Luke 7:28, NKJV.

John Focused on God's Plan:

John's strongest authority was to concentrate on God's plan. He was preaching and preparing people's hearts for the Messiah. John realized God had chosen him and given him a unique task to perform.

He humbled himself with extraordinary obedience to bring the mission to completion. By his messages to prepare the way of the Lord.

He remained faithful and lived with the purity and courage of God's purpose. He was willing to take every part of his enthusiasm to carry out the mission. Even he was eager to die as a martyr for his boldness and preach the Word to repentance from sin.

When we recognize that God chooses us to a high call and special task for our lives. We can move out by faith to the great work of God with great courage.

We trust and depending on the One who ordained us to finish the race. There can be no better satisfaction or achievement in this world than to experience living in God's purpose. It is rewarding to obey and to serve our God on earth and in heaven.

Jesus the Savior

The Power of God has created all creation and demonstrates the God who is existed. It is God himself who would have to manifest His power. No one has been given authority like the Son of God, Jesus.

He declares the greatness of its Creator. The authority of the Lord Jesus has existed before the foundation of the world. Jesus' power was remarkable in both the worldly and spiritual realms. This is the first scriptural reference to the Trinity, "Us."

"Let Us make man in Our image, according to Our likeness." Genesis. 1:26, NKJV.

We recognize **'three persons in One'** in the New Testament as *the God Father, the God Son, and the God Holy Spirit.* John reveals that the Word became flesh.

"All things were made through Him, and without Him nothing was made that was made" John 1:3, NKJV.

Paul said: by the authority of Jesus that **"And He is before all things, and in Him all things consist."** Colossians 1:17, NKJV.

In acknowledging the authority of Jesus was very powerful during his temporary living in the physical body. It is essential to explain something about the character of Christ. He came down from heaven in the flesh.

Power in the Name of Jesus:

Even though he continued his perfect eternal character as the Son of God. He chose to obey the Father to be a servant. The power and the authority have given to Jesus from the Father.

He shall be called: "Anointed One" to bring New Life and miracles to the world. When the Jewish rulers confronted Jesus' authority, they didn't believe Christ, who declares himself as the Savior.

They pointed out that they are waiting to meet the One who is coming soon to save them. Let's confess that Jesus has full spiritual authority over our lives in this world.

We are looking at Jesus as our King and Lord. His grace must humble us to know Him through His Word. He empowered us in His name.

God has offered us the wonderful Name of Jesus to have authority over every evil spirit. The Powerful Name of Jesus is above every name.

We experience the Name in heaven, on earth, and under the earth. All creatures, angels, humankind, and beasts must bow down under the Name of Jesus.

It allows us to use His Name. The power is in His Name! In the Name of Jesus, Amen!

"who being the brightness of His glory and the express image of His person, and upholding

all things by the word of His power" Hebrews 1:3, NKJV.

Salvation and Ministry:

The Word said: Jesus is the Only Way to everlasting salvation, which is why the Father established a plan to send Jesus to save all humankind.

Let's look at how Jesus has come to the world as a baby to save us all and give us life on earth and in heaven. According to the Word, God reached down his love for his creation through the birth of Jesus.

Jesus' genealogy can be found back in the house of David. When we believe that Jesus is Lord. It means that the Son of God accepted physical form in the flesh "Incarnate," dwell among His people.

Jesus was born in Bethlehem; they recorded his life and his ministry in the New Testament. During the reign of Herod, he sought to kill Jesus by assigning all male babies to be killed.

"Now after Jesus was born in Bethlehem of Judea in the days of Herod the king, behold, wise men from the East came to Jerusalem." Matthew 2:1, NKJV.

But an angel appeared to Joseph to take Mary and the baby to Egypt. Then he moved back after Herod's death. They lived in the city of Nazareth in Galilee. There will be a wonderful biography recorded about Jesus' brief life.

The Birth of Jesus:

We are looking at the most powerful birth that ever was and forever will be. It is the birth of Jesus Christ. As the Father had prepared a plan to send His only Son, Jesus, to us as a human form.

Therefore, He came down from heaven in the flesh, as the Bible would call a man. The word incarnation means *"in the flesh."* The precise evidence of the Bible reveals to us that Jesus is God.

The birth of Jesus is truly a mystery. It's unbelievable to many people and significant to other religions around the world.

There may not be discovered in our present time an understanding of how the ways of God will be. It simply can be explained by the revelation of the Spirit of God.

His Birth Planned:

Many scholars suggest that the childbirth of Jesus took place around 7 or 5 BC. The Bible reveals to us, God has chosen that Jesus' birth in His perfect time in the record.

He had confirmed that humanity would have a Savior, and God realized that the world desired love and forgiveness. So, He provided a solution to humankind through the Savior's arrival.

God had organized everything to deliver the Savior. The birth of Jesus would manifest to us that He came to die and bring life to humans. He would give His life for us.

Angel Appeared to Mary:

The angel Gabriel was appointed to meet with Mary, and it was quite frightening for her. The Spirit of God visited her through an angel to inform her. She had been chosen to give birth to the Savior of the world.

Mary was already shocked until Gabriel informed her that she had found favor with God. Gabriel pointed out to her that she would conceive a baby by the power of the Holy Spirit.

Place of His Birth:

We, as believers, celebrate Jesus' birth, but it was a very natural birth. He had to be born in a manger, and God knew that His Son would be special.

Jesus as Savior and He became a servant of humanity throughout history. The prophecies declared that Jesus must be born in Bethlehem of Judea in the time of Herod the King.

"Now after Jesus was born in Bethlehem of Judea in the days of Herod the king, behold, wise men from the East came to Jerusalem." Matthew 2:1, NKJV.

Joseph and Mary traveled from Nazareth to Bethlehem. This journey required them to move down from north to south as a requirement for the census. The authorities were counting people as a requirement for collecting taxes.

The prophecy of the Word explained that the Messiah would come from the tribe of Judah. God fulfilled His covenant that Jesus, the Messiah, would come through the offspring of King David.

The Kingdom of Jesus would never end, and it shall be an everlasting kingdom.

The Ministry of Jesus:

The baby Jesus grew up and matured. He became powerful in Godly character, and the anointing of God was on Him. Jesus increased in knowledge and wisdom, in favor with God and man.

Jesus lived on the earth as the Son of Man in the form of a man; Jesus was surely a human being. He has tempted in all kinds of mortal attacks the same ways that we are now.

But He never committed a sin against His Father. When Jesus identified that His ministry would begin soon. He declared Himself as the Savior in many situations. He came to do the will of God with passion as a servant of God.

Jesus in Temple:

It's described that Jesus was a 12-year-old. He attended with his parents on a trip to Jerusalem, and they became separated from each other. They found Him several days afterward in a temple, a place of worship.

He was explaining some questions to some elders of the temple. Throughout Jesus' life with true evidence that he was working as a carpenter with Joseph. It should prepare him to be sent out to preach the message of Salvation.

It is believed that God set up his ministry at age 30. When he met John Baptist, he baptized Him in Jordan River. He acknowledged him as He is the Son of God.

After Jesus got baptized, God led into the desert to fast for 40 days. Then, Satan came to tempt Jesus three times. Jesus resisted his temptations, and then he left Him alone.

Opposition Rose Against Jesus:

Jesus went on teaching about the kingdom of God. The flocks became greater, and the people declare him as the son of David and as Savior.

The Pharisees found out about Jesus; they wanted to accuse Him of carrying the power of the devil.

He justified his plans with a short story, and later, He challenged them with their own philosophy mentality. He explained to them such understanding but still rejecting the authority of God.

Jesus Asked His Disciples:

When Jesus and His disciples arrived near the city of Caesarea Philippi, Jesus spoke with his disciples. He asked them:

"When Jesus came into the region of Caesarea Philippi, He asked His disciples, saying, "Who do men say that I, the Son of Man, am?" Matthew 16:13, NKJV.

Some of His disciples didn't know how to answer this question? Only Peter answered, saying,

"Simon Peter answered and said, "You are the Christ, the Son of the living God." Matthew 16:16, NKJV.

Jesus told this statement was a supernatural revelation from God. Then, the Lord declared Peter to be the head of the church. He later informed his disciples of the Pharisees' plot against Him.

The plan of the Father allows Him to go through pain and suffering on the cross. Through Him, we may have life in this world and everlasting life with Jesus.

Jesus Revealed Himself:

Jesus reached out to His performance in the cities and villages of Galilee. Many of the ordinary crowd's people cheerfully received Him. But Jesus spoke pure messages from God, and He provoked resistance by the Jewish elders and rulers.

When Jesus was speaking, He offered to tempt them with their clever questions. Some of them did not accept Him with the Jewish doctrine of the law of Moses.

Jesus revealed Himself to them that He is the Messiah. But He advised them to tell nobody about this news. Jesus returned to His homeland. He stated to His disciples that He was planning to fulfill His mission.

Jesus Transfigured on the Mount:

Later on, Jesus chose three of his disciples and took them to a high mountain. Jesus transfigured before His disciples, His face appeared shining like the sun, and his full clothes shone like a white bright.

"and He was transfigured before them. His face shone like the sun, and His clothes became

as white as the light. And behold, Moses and Elijah appeared to them, talking with Him.” Matthew 17:2-3, NKJV.

Suddenly, Moses and Elijah showed up, and Jesus spoke with them.

“While he was still speaking, behold, a bright cloud overshadowed them; and suddenly a voice came out of the cloud, saying, “This is My beloved Son, in whom I am well pleased. Hear Him!” Matthew 17:5, NKJV.

It recognizes as the Transfiguration is an essential stage in Christian doctrine. It further presents Jesus as the Son of the living God.

He Entered Jerusalem:

Jesus entered Jerusalem before the feast of Passover; He was riding on a donkey. Many people followed Him; they picked up palm branches and approached him at the city's entrance.

People honored him as the Son of David and as the Son of God. The priests and leaders of Pharisees were afraid of the rising public applause. They expected something that needed to be done to stop this man and to arrest Him.

"And when He had come into Jerusalem, all the city was moved, saying, "Who is this?" So, the multitudes said, "This is Jesus, the prophet from Nazareth of Galilee." Matthew 21:10-11, NKJV.

Jesus' Final Hours:

When Jesus' final hour in Jerusalem approaches, it describes in all four Gospels. As it's recorded, Jesus performed signs and wonders and healing during his ministry.

He performed a miracle to raise Lazarus from the dead to life. He opposed the business market sale dealers in the temple. The high priests asked him who gave him the authority to do these things:

"and spoke to Him, saying, "Tell us, by what authority are You doing these things? Or who is he who gave You this authority?" Luke 20:2, NKJV.

He informed his disciples about the forthcoming days it would destroy the temple in Jerusalem. At the same time, elders and the chief priests reached an agreement to meet with a high priest Caiaphas.

They planned to arrest Jesus. They used one of Jesus' disciples; Judas was willing to betray Him to show the chief priests to where Jesus is? He said; how he would hand over Jesus to them. They admitted offering him 30 pieces of silver.

The Last Supper:

When Jesus and His twelve disciples were gathered for Passover meal together. He did his final speeches of teaching. The Passover meal arranged to celebrate, to be remembered as a Feast of the Lord.

The Messiah would free Israel, not from captivity in Egypt this time, but from the bondage of sin.

Jesus is the Savior, and those who believe in Him shall receive the salvation of the Lord. He also referred to that one of them would betray him.

Jesus quietly wanted to let Judas recognize it, as he who would hand Jesus over to the chief priests to be crucified. Jesus informed Peter that before a rooster crowed, he would deny Him three times.

At the end of the supper, Jesus established the Christian ceremony known as "Holy Communion." We will bless the bread as Jesus' body and wine as the blood. It's broken and shared for all. It establishes a new covenant between God and man.

Jesus Arrested:

After Jesus finished the Last Supper with his disciples, he left for the Garden of Gethsemane to pray. Jesus prayed to His Father in asking if this cup could be taken away from him.

He urged all of his disciples to pray with him, but they continued falling asleep. Suddenly, the hour had come when the chief priests and their Soldiers arrived to arrest Jesus. Judas was among them and pointed out Jesus with a kiss.

One of the disciples attacked to prevent the arrest was cutting the ear off one of the soldiers. But Jesus rebuked him and restored the soldier's ear.

Brought Jesus on the Trial:

Many of the disciples saw what happened to Jesus; then they took off to hide themselves.

They took Jesus away by soldiers to the high priest to ask questions as a typical convicted on trial.

Meanwhile, someone in the crowd identified Peter and repeatedly asked him if he was one of Jesus' disciples. Each time, Peter denied it, and then a rooster crowed. Then they moved Jesus outside of the court, and He looked straight at Peter.

He reminded that Jesus had told him he would deny Him three times, and he went to weep bitterly. Judas, who was observing from a far distance, saw what was happening to Jesus.

He regretted turning Jesus over, not realizing the harshness of his act, and tried to return the 30 pieces of silver. The priests said his sin and his guilt were his own responsibility.

Judas realized he had betrayed an innocent man, threw the coins into the temple, and went to hang himself.

The Crucifixion:

The next day, they brought in Jesus to the high court where they insulted and beat Him.

They convicted Him that Jesus claimed to be the Son of God.

Confirming to the truths of the Word. The entire assault against Jesus was that He declared Himself as the king of the Jews.

The Roman guards had mocked Him; they put on him in a purple robe and place a crown of thorns on his head. The priests and Elders demanded that he should be sentenced to death on the cross.

Then they took him before Pontius Pilate. He was ruling as a Roman governor of Judea. In the beginning, Pilate decided to let Jesus go and sent Him to King Herod.

But the people were insisting he be condemned to death. Pilate said to the Jewish priests he could find no wrongdoing Jesus had committed.

The priests pointed out to him that anybody who declared to be a king goes against Caesar. So, Pilate chose to wash his hands of this act in public, letting the people decide.

The Roman soldiers beat and struck Jesus; they put a crown of thorns on his head. They took Him outside Jerusalem on a hill called Golgotha to be crucified.

Jesus on the Cross:

In evidence of crucifixion was a Roman style of executing a convicted criminal. So, they crucified Jesus with two other felons, one man at his left and the other man at his right.

Above his head was a sign that was written; **"King of the Jews."** They were other people, the mother of Jesus Mary and Mary Magdalene, among those people watching the crucifixion of Jesus.

The Gospels tell extraordinary incidents that took place during those hours on the cross. One of the thieves was with Jesus on the cross.

"Then he said to Jesus, "Lord, remember me when You come into Your kingdom." And Jesus said to him, "Assuredly, I say to you, today you will be with Me in Paradise." Luke 23:42-43, NKJV.

Jesus gave up his spirit, and shortly upon his death. The black sky and an earthquake exploded. At that moment, the curtain of the temple's

Veil was splitting from top to bottom. The earth shook, and the rocks split.

"Then, behold, the veil of the temple was torn in two from top to bottom; and the earth quaked, and the rocks were split." Matthew 27:51, NKJV.

To confirm his death, one of the soldiers pierced Jesus' side with a spear, bringing a sudden flow of blood and water.

"But one of the soldiers pierced His side with a spear, and immediately blood and water came out." John 19:34, NKJV.

After Jesus's death on the cross took Him down and wrapped his body in a linen cloth. Then, Joseph put him in the tomb.

"Then he bought fine linen, took Him down, and wrapped Him in the linen. And he laid Him in a tomb which had been hewn out of the rock, and rolled a stone against the door of the tomb." Mark 15:46, NKJV.

He is Risen:

The most significant factor in humankind's history is the resurrection of Jesus. God manifested His power and His authority to demonstrate all events. From the beginning, God had a plan to manifest His power to resurrect His Son. As suddenly, the tomb broke up.

"and the graves were opened; and many bodies of the saints who had fallen asleep were raised." Matthew 27:52, NKJV.

Then, on the third day, the power of God raised Him from the dead; the victory is won. The resurrection of Jesus is completed by the power of God alone. He is alive.

Suffering and pain on a cross were turned into true joy. They found Jesus' tomb was empty. The angel of the Lord showed up inside the tomb to Mary Magdalene and his mother, Mary. So, they left the tomb to find all disciples to inform them.

"And entering the tomb, they saw a young man clothed in a long white robe sitting on the right side; and they were alarmed." Mark 16:5, NKJV.

Jesus appeared to all of His disciples, who were hiding from the Romans. He told them not to be frightened.

Jesus Ascended into Heaven:

The time came for Jesus' ascension back into heaven to the Father after forty days of resurrection.

As we know, Jesus brought his disciples to Mount Olive on the east side of Jerusalem. Jesus said his final messages to them and encouraged them to wait upon the promise of the Father.

He instructed them with a Great Commission to go around the world and preach and teach the gospel to all mankind.

"Go, therefore and make disciples of all the nations, baptizing them in the name of the Father and of the Son and of the Holy Spirit," Matthew 28:19, NKJV.

He will send the Holy Spirit to receive the power to witness the Good News. Then, he was taken high on a cloud and ascended into heaven.

"Now it came to pass, while He blessed them, that He was parted from them and carried up into heaven." Luke 24:51, NKJV.

Encouraged us to Witness:

Jesus encouraged His disciples to proclaim the Gospel and to preach the eternal salvation to the entire world. He is the Son of God, the Messiah. Their work of the Kingdom would be a triumph.

It will give the highest reward when they continued to be faithful in the work of God and surrendered themselves to the will of God.

Jesus worked with signs and wonders to demonstrate the One True God. He instructed them to declare the love of God to all nations. May they preach the Word and to invite them to a new life and to offer them God's grace.

I believe Jesus gave us all the authority and the power of His glory to preach His Word of salvation. He commanded us to heal the sick in their bodies and to those who need the Savior in Jesus' name. Amen.

Death and Resurrection

It describes the Christian cross as a sign of the crucifixion of Jesus for us. The cross is a divine bridge between God's love and humanity. His perfect justification fulfilled at the cross.

The meaning of the cross in Christianity would be a terrible death achieved by the willingness of Jesus. He brought down the grace of God from heaven and provided a unique life for mankind.

Because Jesus knew what would take place on the cross. He had to obey the Father and sacrifice His own life for the sake of humankind.

By His atoning sacrifice on the cross, Jesus was filled with pain and suffering. It would allow us to have faith, forgiveness, salvation, and eternal life.

He was born to die for our sins so that we might have a new relationship with the Father again.

Crucified with Christ:

The cross of Jesus is essential in the Christian doctrine. The cross demonstrates the work of God's plan for salvation from start to finish.

God gave His only Son to reveal that His character, His compassion, His love. His justice had been accomplished by the obedience of Jesus on the cross.

However, Jesus called His disciples to pick up their own crosses and follow Him daily. We need to stand strong in a challenging time and be faithful to carry our own cross. This means that we will die in ourselves and in our flesh to follow Him.

"I have been crucified with Christ; it is no longer I who live, but Christ lives in me; and the life which I now live in the flesh I live by faith in the Son of God, who loved me and gave Himself for me." Galatians 2:20, NKJV.

Death on the Cross:

If there were no death on the cross by Jesus, there would not be a new life for us. To carry the cross means that we will pick up our cross to follow Jesus. There are many places in the world where Christians are persecuted strongly because of their faith.

We must recognize what it means to carry our cross and follow Jesus in a profoundly genuine way. Jesus prayed to the Father on the cross.

"He went a little farther and fell on His face, and prayed, saying, "O My Father, if it is possible, let this cup pass from Me; nevertheless, not as I will, but as You will." Matthew 26:39, NKJV.

What if there was a time when Jesus could have passed up the crucifixion by His own flesh?

If Jesus made the wrong decision and had not gone to the cross to die for the world? What would have taken place to us and the world? Would the plan of God have been fulfilled yet?

The Resurrection of Jesus

Jesus is risen; we are now rejoicing in the resurrection of Jesus. This is significant because it shows the awesome power of God. We believe God was working in the time of the resurrection.

We all believe God exists. Our God has the power to create anything and everything according to His will and His pleasure. He has created the universe, and He has power over it.

When Jesus died on the cross, the power of God raised Jesus from the dead to life on the third day. Thus, He has the authority to raise the dead.

Power over the Death:

God has authority and power over death; He is worthy of our confidence and prayers. He alone who established the living soul can resurrect it from death to life.

God was in control over Jesus, even from the grave. God now admonishes us of His everlasting supremacy over life and death.

We can look at another powerful justification for this act of God. The resurrection of Jesus is correct, and it testifies to His sinless nature and holy character. Jesus never sinned, and He was born sinless. Paul preached, based on the resurrection of Christ.

"Therefore let it be known to you, brethren, that through this Man is preached to you the forgiveness of sins; and by Him everyone who believes is justified from all things from which you could not be justified by the law of Moses." Acts 13:38-39, NKJV.

Evidence of His Resurrection:

The resurrection of Jesus is the evidence of His divinity. It also confirms the Old Testament revelation that prophesied of Jesus' resurrection.

"This Jesus whom I preach to you is the Christ." Acts 17:3, NKJV.

Jesus' resurrection proves He was raised on the third day. And if Jesus has not risen from death, then we have no truth and no confidence in our hearts.

Without the evidence of Jesus' resurrection, our life is meaningless. Without the Savior, there will not be any salvation and no eternal life. Jesus said;

"I am the resurrection and the life." John 11:25, NKJV.

Victorious Resurrection:

The resurrection of Jesus is the glorious and victorious testimony for every Christian believer.

"For I delivered to you first of all that which I also received: that Christ died for our sins according to the Scriptures, and that He was buried, and that He rose again the third day according to the Scriptures." 1 Corinthians 15:3-4, NKJV.

The resurrection of Jesus is truly remarkable. It shows us who Jesus is. It proves that God has fulfilled His promise to sacrifice His only Son, Jesus, on our behalf.

The Word confirms that the mighty power of God is present to raise us from the dead. It affirms that the bodies of those who trust in Jesus will not be forgotten but will be resurrected unto everlasting life. He is coming back again!

"For the Lord Himself will descend from heaven with a shout, with the voice of an archangel, and with the trumpet of God. And the dead in Christ will rise first." 1 Thessalonians 4:16, NKJV.

The Four Gospels

WE FIND FOUR GOSPELS in the New Testament: **Matthew, Mark, Luke, and John.** The four books tell of one Gospel, the word gospel meaning "Good News."

Jesus' story is mentioned through the four Gospels of the New Testament. These books record the life of our Savior, Jesus.

Each author was writing the Word of God by the inspiration of the Holy Spirit in the Gospels. Each book reveals the story of the ministry, death, and resurrection of Jesus, the Son of Living God.

Each of them wrote each gospel differently. They were focusing on all kinds of people in different places. They lived with all diverse languages, backgrounds, cultures, and traditions.

They all have distinct interests, written by extraordinary writers who were seeking to achieve a specific task and to fulfill the purpose of God.

He entered into a sinful world, giving a message of hope. He suffered for us to die that we might have eternal life through Him.

Jesus came back to Galilee, and He made some great impact by His public preaching all around cities. During His message and teaching to many people followed him, some people became his disciples.

Many Walked with Him:

All Gospels were written to describe Jesus as these disciples were walking with Him. Then Jesus has chosen twelve disciples out of many followers of Him.

They went through Judea and Galilee; Jesus was teaching many powerful parables to demonstrate how much our Heavenly Father loves us.

He shared the prophecies fulfilled as the teaching of Jesus filling people's hearts with hope. He began to heal the sick and every disease, and more people turned out to follow him.

Jesus walked among the people to serve, and many received Him by a huge number of people.

There, He was preaching on the Mount. He taught with several speeches called; the Beatitudes. The outline of His teaching is related to many of the divine plans of God, love, humbleness, and grace.

Unique Messages:

The original four books of the Gospels are to testify in the time of the preaching, teachings, and healings of Jesus. So, we may know that He is the Son of God and that we declare Him to be the Messiah.

God used individual authors with diverse backgrounds and qualities to send out His messages through their writings. Each of the gospel writers had a special intention behind their faith.

Those chosen servants were carrying out the purposes of God. Every one of them shares the plan of God a unique way in the life and ministry of Jesus.

The Book of Matthew

Matthew was one of the disciples, and he provided an inspiring gospel that tells about our

Savior. He describes an accurate story of the life of Jesus.

Some believe his gospel is the longest of the four gospels, and that's why it was the first story to be recorded.

Matthew's major purpose is to explain to the Jewish people that Jesus is the Messiah. He presents this in his book by showing how Jesus has fulfilled the Old Testament's prophecies.

Matthew had his own business as a tax collector in the city of Capernaum. He was called Levi, the son of Alphaeus. Also, it is not unusual for a man to be given a unique name after an experience with God.

It's a possibility that Jesus changed his name to Matthew from Levi after his transformation. The name Matthew is defined as *"gift of God."* Now when Matthew met Jesus, a new life transformed into his life.

Matthew Tax Collector:

At that time, their society rejected tax collectors. Because they served the Roman authorities and enriched themselves by collecting taxes from their own people. Sometimes they were dishonestly collecting enormous amounts.

Matthew was a tax collector who was recognized by the religious population as a truly disgraceful person. So even spending time with this person could directly destroy a good person's respect.

And yet Jesus was enjoying a meal at Matthew's home, along with other tax collectors and sinners who were presented. The Pharisees confronted the disciples about Jesus visiting new people.

Promised of the Messiah:

The gospel of Matthew tells of the coming of the promised Savior and the Messiah. We learn that Matthew presents Jesus as the King of the Jews. It is evident what the purpose and fulfillment were of Jesus.

He is an extraordinary character in the Scriptures. Matthew shows the spirit of revelation to be fulfilled in Christ. He explains the principle of the law, and God's acting in love to save His people, to fulfill His promise through Christ.

Matthew moves on to present Israel's refusal of their king, and further. He describes God brought the people back together in Christ.

The Book of Mark

The writer of the second gospel is Mark, otherwise known as John Mark. Jesus had appointed him to be a follower. He had a humble character in the New Testament documents.

He had a strong relationship with one of his relatives, Barnabas, who was his cousin. He was one of the leaders of the congregation in Antioch.

Mark followed Paul and Barnabas on one of their evangelistic travels. The gospel of Mark contains high levels of truthfulness in the essential stories of the way of life, disciplines, and teaching of Jesus.

It reflects a truly short gospel compared to all of the other gospels that were presented after it.

Works of Jesus:

Mark was undoubtedly deeply fascinated by the magnificent works of Jesus. He knew that the Lord demonstrated His salvation, and he walked in Jesus' teaching by the fulfillment of God's plan.

More than half of Mark's gospel provides a statement of the wonderful accomplishments that Jesus performed. Including that Jesus surely had healed many sick people.

He provides truthful evidence of the teachings of Jesus to confirm the fundamental Word. Although Jesus was the true Messiah, allowing us to believe and have faith in Jesus. People must hear the Word and to receive salvation.

The Book of Luke

The important portion of the gospel of Luke was recorded. We are informed that many people were eyewitnesses to the truth of the stories of Jesus.

We find that God has chosen Luke to write this book. He was the only Gentile author, a physician, a missionary, a teacher, a doctor.

The Lord changed him into ministry as a pastor, an evangelist, a partner, a brother in Christ. He became a scholar and a humble man of God.

He certainly wrote his gospel with a Gentile audience at heart. He made sure to reveal Jesus' character and His love for the world.

Luke explained the Law:

The Jewish people would have found out they had circumcised Jesus since He was raised in a Jewish family. If it wasn't told, no one could recognize it.

Luke made sure to give an accurate definition of everything. He mentioned so that those who were not as comfortable with Jewish customs and traditional practices.

The Old Testament evidence would find it easy to understand the biography of Jesus and the plan of salvation.

Writing True Evidence:

Luke and some other apostles stood faithful with the apostle Paul to his death. His intention and purpose in telling this truth were to write unique evidence about Jesus. He said what God has designed to be the plan of salvation.

He told of the incredible love of God and the true doctrine. He motivated by the Spirit with

God's instruction what he precisely directed to do.

Luke did not point out in his writing the destruction of the temple in Jerusalem. But it's believed that Luke recorded his gospel before the year 63AD.

Gave up His life for Jesus:

Luke possibly had lived a fascinating way of life in Antioch. He studied medicine, but he preferred to sacrifice himself and give up his life of enjoyment in order to follow the Lord Jesus.

God changed and transformed Luke's life, just as every sinner turns to a new and unique experience. He felt the forgiveness and cleanness of the Lord made him pure by the blood of the Lamb.

He was an ordinary man, as he appeared not to write a gospel for reputation or honor. Because of his humbleness, he preferred not to bring up his name and to be recognized in the book.

Luke wished to instruct people to teach them about the Savior who had already come. To teach about the wonderful redemption of Jesus as He reaches out to all humankind.

The Book of John

The purpose of the gospel of John is to present the truth that Jesus of Nazareth was the Christ. John mentioned with the conviction that Jesus is the Son of God.

John encouraged the followers of the Lord Jesus that they would receive everlasting life. He emphasized the key point in the gospel of John, and that was the eternal Living Word.

"In the beginning was the Word, and the Word was with God, and the Word was God." John 1:1, NKJV.

Jesus became Flash:

The Word became flesh and lived among men in the life of Jesus. John revealed that Jesus appeared of heavenly birth. He referred to Jesus as a bodily being who owned physical flesh and blood.

As the same God, He created us in a human body. The plan of God was very significant that Jesus would come down from heaven. Being obedient under the authority of the Creator God and become human as the incarnation of God.

We believe God can dwell in a human body, that He will give His spirit to us. Then we carry His passion and His love of eternal life in the sinful world.

Two Parts Represent:

John's story of the ministry of Jesus consists of two parts. As we know, many chapters represent Jesus' ministry, starting with His contact with John the Baptist.

The other chapters informed us of the earthly ministry of Jesus when He made a direction to His disciples. He pointed out the purpose of His life and His willingness to approach death.

Revealed the Son of God:

In the gospel of John would tell us a true statement of who Jesus is. John reveals that Jesus is the Son of God that He sent His Son to die for the sins of the world.

"For God so loved the world that He gave His only begotten Son, that whoever believes

in Him should not perish but have everlasting life." John 3:16, NKJV.

Before the crucifixion of Jesus on the cross, Jesus manifested God's perfect character of generous love.

He challenged His disciples to work profound actions of love as they cared for others with an unselfish heart.

Jesus Performed Miracles:

The Bible indicates thirty-seven phenomena with signs and wonders and especially healings. Jesus performed many miracles during the three years of His ministry.

These miracles took place through His presence on the earth. As He walked with His disciples and healed all sickness and raised dead bodies to life.

We will praise and honor Jesus for many miracles of healing He has done. His miracles and healings appear to improve the lives of people, as the Word would testify.

Let's look at the details of these *thirty-seven miracles of Jesus.* We must recognize that these are entirely the marvelous miracles that are reported.

Thirty-Seven Miracles and Healings of Jesus

It sounds like Jesus had related to the event in Cana. Jesus might have preferred this house to perform His first miracle; He turned water into wine.

It was a typical location where Jesus came to show the miracles of God by His glorious power. He may want us to learn from the supernatural work of Jesus in a wedding event.

"This beginning of signs Jesus did in Cana of Galilee, and manifested His glory; and His disciples believed in Him." John 2:11, NKJV.

Jesus healed a certain royal official man's son who was very sick. He went to Jesus and begged Him to heal his son. Jesus encouraged him that his son would live.

The Bible mentioned that the man took Jesus' word by faith, and he departed. His son received healing at the very hour Jesus told him.

"Then he inquired of them the hour when he got better. And they said to him, "Yesterday at

the seventh hour the fever left him."** John 4:52, NKJV.

Jesus cast out demons just with a word; we see the demons talked back to Jesus. He said to demons, "Be quiet!" "Come out of him!"

"saying, "Let us alone! What have we to do with You, Jesus of Nazareth? Did You come to destroy us? I know who You are—the Holy One of God!" Mark 1:24, NKJV.

A man had suffered leprosy, and no one would allow themselves to touch the man. But when he saw Jesus, he fell on his knees and worshiped the Lord.

"And behold, a leper came and worshiped Him, saying, "Lord, if You are willing, You can make me clean." Matthew 8:2, NKJV.

Jesus arrived at Peter's house to heal his mother-in-law; she had become very sick of a fever.

"Now when Jesus had come into Peter's house, He saw his wife's mother lying sick with a fever. So He touched her hand, and the fever left her. And she arose and served them." Matthew 8:14-15, NKJV.

Jesus had the authority to cast out evil spirits in the evening. Jesus healed many sick people.

"When evening had come, they brought to Him many who were demon-possessed. And He cast out the spirits with a word, and healed all who were sick." Matthew 8:16, NKJV.

Jesus asked His disciples to watch His first miraculous catch of fish. They then chose to trust and live by His Word. I believe it was a good exercise for all of the disciples on the Lake of Gennesaret to understand how to obey His Word.

"For he and all who were with him were astonished at the catch of fish which they had taken." Luke 5:9, NKJV.

Jesus quickly reached out His hand and touched him, saying, "Be clean." And instantly, leprosy left him.

"Then He put out His hand and touched him, saying, "I am willing; be cleansed." Immediately the leprosy left him." Luke 5:13, NKJV.

We see the dynamic faith of the centurion in Capernaum. He was an expert officer of the Roman army, and when Jesus saw his faith. He requested Jesus to restore his paralyzed servant.

"Then Jesus said to the centurion, "Go your way; and as you have believed, so let it be done for you." And his servant was healed that same hour." Matthew 8:13, NKJV.

Jesus has the power to forgive sins and to heal a paralyzed man. No matter what sickness we have or what sins we have committed, He heals and forgives us. He has the power given from heaven to heal us.

"But that you may know that the Son of Man has power on earth to forgive sins"—then He said to the paralytic, "Arise, take up your bed, and go to your house." Matthew 9:6, NKJV.

Jesus even has the power to heal a man's shriveled hand on the Sabbath. He believed in His mighty power and received healing. He can heal any kind of sickness right now.

"But He knew their thoughts, and said to the man who had the withered hand, "Arise and stand here." And he arose and stood." Luke 6:8, NKJV.

Jesus raised a widow's son from the dead. In this case, people were walking with the widow and the dead body of a young man.

The unexpected arrival of Jesus to the town brought a supernatural miracle raising the young man from death to life. Glory to His name.

"So he who was dead sat up and began to speak. And He presented him to his mother." Luke 7:15, NKJV.

Jesus calmed the storm. We can recognize the storms of life as we live in the middle of the attacks of the enemy every day. We believe and trust Jesus to stop the storms of life and bring His peace over us.

"But He said to them, "Why are you so fearful? How is it that you have no faith?" Mark 4:40, NKJV.

Jesus commanded that the demons come out of a demon-possessed man and pass into a herd of pigs. All the demons recognized Jesus, and they obeyed Him, even as they asked for permission to leave the man alone. **The demons begged Jesus**.

"So all the demons begged Him, saying, "Send us to the swine, that we may enter them." Mark 5:12, NKJV.

A woman had a disease for twelve years, and no physicians could restore her.

No one had not been given her any hope, but when she came to Jesus. She reached out and touched Jesus' robe.

"And He said to her, "Daughter, your faith has made you well. Go in peace, and be healed of your affliction." Mark 5:34, NKJV.

Jesus raised the synagogue leader's daughter back to life after she had died.

God was working among His people to do wonders through Jesus.

"He said to them, "Make room, for the girl is not dead, but sleeping." And they ridiculed Him." Matthew 9:24, NKJV.

Jesus healed two blind men, restoring their sight—not only their natural eyesight, but they also received a fresh faith and a new insight of Jesus.

"Then He touched their eyes, saying, "According to your faith let it be to you." Matthew 9:29, NKJV.

Jesus healed a man who had demon-possessed, he who couldn't talk. The Word of God said that the crowd was amazed.

"And when the demon was cast out, the mute spoke. And the multitudes marveled, saying, "It was never seen like this in Israel!" Matthew 9:33, NKJV.

Jesus met many men lying by the pool of Bethesda, who needed healing. He said to one of them.

"Jesus said to him, "Rise, take up your bed and walk." And immediately the man was made well, took up his bed, and walked. And that day was the Sabbath." John 5:8-9, NKJV.

The healing of Jesus had been wonderfully significant, and every man can now receive healing in any place. He is the healer of all sickness. The Bible tells us that later Jesus found the man at the temple and said to him.

"Afterward Jesus found him in the temple, and said to him, "See, you have been made well. Sin no more, lest a worse thing come upon you." John 5:14, NKJV.

When a crowd of five thousand people desired for food. They asked a young boy for his lunch; he had five loaves of bread and two fishes. Jesus gave thanks.

The bread was amazingly multiplied so that all disciples served all the crowds, and they gathered twelve baskets full leftover.

"Then He took the five loaves and the two fish, and looking up to heaven, He blessed and broke them, and gave them to the disciples to set before the multitude." Luke 9:16, NKJV.

Jesus performed another wonder by walking on water; He had declared to the storm to be quiet.

"for they all saw Him and were troubled. But immediately He talked with them and said to them, "Be of good cheer! It is I; do not be afraid." Mark 6:50, NKJV.

People showed up in the crowds with great faith to touch His garment in order to be healed. What powerful healing Jesus had to be able to release His healing through His garment. Glory to His name!

"and begged Him that they might only touch the hem of His garment. And as many as touched it were made perfectly well." Matthew 14:36, NKJV.

Jesus healed a Gentile woman's demon-possessed daughter. She begged Jesus to cast out the devil from her daughter's life.

She was a Greek, not a Jewish woman. Jesus knew she had a strong faith. He said to her that your daughter would be fine.

"Then He said to her, "For this saying go your way; the demon has gone out of your daughter." Mark 7:29, NKJV.

Jesus' compassion for the multitude caused him to feed 4,000 people with seven loaves and fishes. Anywhere Jesus walked among people, His presence served as the Bread of Life.

That's why crowds were following Him to receive eternal life because He is the Bread of Life.

"So they all ate and were filled, and they took up seven large baskets full of the fragments that were left. Now those who ate were four thousand men, besides women and children." Matthew 15:37-38, NKJV.

Jesus healed a blind man at Bethsaida. They begged Jesus to touch the blind man to restore his eyesight. The man experienced with one-touch of Jesus; he will receive his vision back.

"Then He put His hands on his eyes again and made him look up. And he was restored and saw everyone clearly." Mark 8:25, NKJV.

Jesus healed a man born blind by putting mud on his eyes. People brought in a blind man, and Jesus used the mud to touch and create new sight for the blind man. He healed his sight.

Faith can move the mountain if we release our faith to see the impossible work of God. He can transform from the natural to the supernatural.

"When He had said these things, He spat on the ground and made clay with the saliva; and He anointed the eyes of the blind man with the clay. And He said to him, "Go, wash in the pool of Siloam" (which is translated, Sent). So he went and washed, and came back seeing." John 9:6-7, NKJV.

Jesus healed a demon-possessed boy. He had mercy on the people even though His disciples couldn't cast the demons out of the boy's life.

"And Jesus rebuked the demon, and it came out of him; and the child was cured from that very hour." Matthew 17:18, NKJV.

Jesus healed another blind man. We know that a devil can cause someone to be mute because of a demonic presence in his life.

Jesus had the power and the anointing of healing to restore every man who reached out to Him. He would not reject anyone.

"Then one was brought to Him who was demon-possessed, blind and mute; and He healed him, so that the [a]blind and mute man both spoke and saw." Matthew 12:22, NKJV.

There was a woman who had crippled for eighteen years, then Jesus healed her on the Sabbath. God will move anytime and anywhere, even among those who are not believers. The people overjoyed all the magnificent works of God that Jesus was doing.

"And He laid His hands on her, and immediately she was made straight, and glorified God." Luke 13:13, NKJV.

Jesus healed a man with dropsy, which is the abnormal swelling of the body, and He did so on the Sabbath. Jesus was at a Pharisee's house, where He healed someone who suffered from this disease in his body.

All the people marveled to see the glory of God performed in such a way.

"But they kept silent. And He took him and healed him, and let him go." Luke 14:4, NKJV.

Jesus healed ten men who had leprosy while on His way back to their city, Jerusalem, but one of them was a Samaritan. That one came back to thank Jesus for healing him.

"And one of them, when he saw that he was healed, returned, and with a loud voice glorified God, and fell down on his face at His feet, giving Him thanks. And he was a Samaritan." Luke 17:15-16, NKJV.

Jesus raised Lazarus from the dead. Lazarus fell sick in Bethany, and his sisters asked Jesus to come to see him. Jesus knew that Lazarus was "sleeping," and that the death of Lazarus would bring glory and praise to God.

He waited four days to come to see them, and when He went to Lazarus. He realized that Lazarus was already dead. He could have just sent a word to heal him, but He didn't do that.

Jesus wanted to reveal God's power in front of people at the graveside. He knew that by His presence, Lazarus should be resurrected again. God shall be magnified and glorified.

"Now when He had said these things, He cried with a loud voice, "Lazarus, come forth!" And he who had died came out bound hand and foot with graveclothes, and his face was wrapped with a cloth. Jesus said to them, Loose him, and let him go." John 11:43-44, NKJV.

Blind Bartimaeus received his sight when Jesus passed by in Jericho. Bartimaeus heard that Jesus was around, and although he couldn't see. But he could feel it, and he had the faith to shout out to Jesus to restore his sight.

"Then Jesus said to him, "Go your way; your faith has made you well." And immediately he received his sight and followed Jesus on the road." Mark 10:52, NKJV.

Jesus cursed a fig tree on the road from Bethany. Jesus had such power from on high over nature that the tree withered. Jesus said that it would never bear fruit again.

"And seeing a fig tree by the road, He came to it and found nothing on it but leaves, and said to it, "Let no fruit grow on you ever

again." **Immediately the fig tree withered away."** Matthew 21:19, NKJV.

Jesus' time had arrived to be arrested. When one of the disciples saw the servant of the high priest in the crowd come to take Jesus into custody. The disciple cut off the man's right ear. Jesus simply placed the man's ear back onto his face and healed him.

"And one of them struck the servant of the high priest and cut off his right ear. But Jesus answered and said, "Permit even this." And He touched his ear and healed him." Luke 22:50-51, NKJV.

The second miracle that Jesus performed was that of the catching of fish at sea.

Jesus multiplied much fish and supplied their needs. What wonderful miracles we experience when we seek Jesus for provision. He will always provide for us.

"Simon Peter went up and dragged the net to land, full of large fish, one hundred and fifty-three; and although there were so many, the net was not broken." John 21:11, NKJV.

Jesus paid a tax to the temple through a coin found in a fish's mouth. What a the miracle was that Jesus knew there would be a coin in the mouth of that fish, He said to Peter.

"Nevertheless, lest we offend them, go to the sea, cast in a hook, and take the fish that comes up first. And when you have opened its mouth, you will find a piece of money; take that and give it to them for Me and you." Matthew 17:27, NKJV.

Jesus still Heals His people:

People brought many kinds of infirmities to Jesus, and He healed them all. Jesus chose twelve men, and He taught them how to cast devils out of people's lives.

He showed them how to use His power and authority to stand strong over devils. He assigned these disciples the mission to preach the kingdom of God. He anointed them to heal the sick.

His popularity reached everywhere, and people were rejoicing as great crowds came simultaneously to listen to Him. He taught them with the Word, and people came ready to receive healing from their diseases. Amen.

The Book of Acts

AS THE BOOK OF Acts opens, we see the ascension of Jesus with a great victory. He should be returning to the Father; Jesus told His disciples. He promised them that He would send back the Holy Spirit to the earth.

His presence would continue to be with His disciples. Acts 2 tells of the experiences of the Day of Pentecost.

All the disciples were waiting to receive more power to stand strong in their faith. Because they were very frightened to reach out and be a witness of Jesus.

The Day of Pentecost:

As they gathered together, the Holy Spirit came like a rushing wind over all the disciples. They were filled with the Spirit. The Holy Spirit baptized them with a new language and empowered them to be witnesses of Jesus.

They were excited and able to preach the Gospel boldly. The Lord Jesus began to anoint them with a new fresh outpouring of His Spirit. Then the Holy Spirit empowered them to move forward.

They gave the testimony of His Good News, many giving witness by their lifestyles of holiness.

The Acts of the Apostles:

The Book of Acts is the excellent work of God's servants and how they proclaimed the kingdom of God. The Acts of the Apostles is a wonderful book in the Bible.

They made the true witness of the apostles who were entrusted with the living Holy Spirit upon their lives.

It reveals how the disciples of Jesus moved on after Jesus' ascension to heaven. When He was not there physically with them, they kept their confidence in the Lord and did not quit very easily.

Instead, they put their faith and hope in Jesus. They were so persuaded by Jesus' instructions, teachings, and miracle-working wonders. They kept preaching and experiencing the

positive message even at enormous life-threat-
ening risks to themselves!

Not Silent for Preaching:

The early disciples were very strong in the
Spirit, and even though they faced a lot of persecution. But they did not go silent in their
messages!

The story of Acts tells how the early congregation increased in great numbers in Jerusalem.
Later it was expanded into the neighboring region of Judea. God moved in the middle of all
the crises in the lives of the apostles.

One of them, the missionary Philip, brought
the glorious news of Jesus, about His death
and resurrection. It caused a revival, took place
among the people of Samaria.

Congregation Grown:

Sometimes the early Church was growing,
and great numbers of believers were being
added to the congregation. All the apostles were
preaching the Gospel. God wanted the apostle
Peter to preach the Gospel to the Gentiles.

There was a Roman soldier named Cornelius; he was a God-fearing Gentile. Cornelius had an experience with God.

He prayed to the God of Israel, but he recognized nothing about the God of salvation. Later, he found out about Jesus, who is the Jewish Messiah.

Gospel Preaches to all People:

The Lord called Peter to witness to Cornelius and his family. Peter preached the Word to them, and the Holy Spirit came upon Cornelius's family and made them new believers in Christ.

So, the Lord Jesus had revealed to Peter that the Gospel was not only for the Jewish people. But it was for all people, even Gentiles, and around the world.

I would say that the Book of Acts tells a series of the Acts of the Apostles. It reviews the ministry of the apostles with their power and passion and excitement to proclaim the Good News!

I normally suggest to people that they go into their Bible study by reading first the four gospels in the New Testament. Then by reading the Acts of the Apostles.

Apostles Continued Serving:

In many situations, we can most certainly prove the Acts of the Apostles. Because they are the most interesting stories from the Word of God.

The list of these excellent men of God in the record of Acts shows that they came from widely diverse backgrounds.

It included these servants of God in the biblical record: *Peter, Paul, James, Timothy, John, Stephen, Philip, Ananias, Barnabas, James, Titus, Luke, and more...*

These apostles were the disciples of Jesus first. Then they continued to testify after the ascension of Jesus under the leadership of the Holy Spirit. Amen.

The Apostle Paul

The Word of God stated that throughout Paul's writings and his entire ministry. He was a zealous man; he had a great enthusiasm to preach the love of Jesus. He had a personal visitation with the Lord Jesus.

He had an original name, Saul, but the Lord changed his name to Paul after his conversion.

Because he was to be identified as a passionate follower of the Lord Jesus.

I wish we all could be like Paul. As we recognize, he came from the tribe of Benjamin, and he presented himself as a Jew.

He came from a Hebrew background, passing on to the Mosaic Law as found in the first five books of the Old Testament and including the Ten Commandments.

Between the Pharisees and the Sadducees:

His story brings about the differences between the Pharisees and the Sadducees through the Scriptures.

The Sadducees denied a concept of the resurrection of the dead. But the Pharisees appeared to agree on the resurrection.

The Sadducees accepted the Hebrew Bible but rejected the instructions of the Pharisees in connection with the experience that observed the Bible and oral law.

"The deity and spirit of the Oral Law as passed on from God to Moses on Mount Sinai."

Sadducees denied the doctrine of any kind of existence after death, but the Pharisees recognize a resurrection, and angels, demons, heaven, and hell...

Paul had Conversion:

Paul had a sincere heart to persecute the early Church, as he was carrying his faith according to the law. He was to turn into one of the best Christian missionaries of his time.

He reached many people with the Gospel after he had an experience with Jesus on the way to Damascus. Before his conversion, Paul considered what he could do to attack and break down the rise of Christianity.

Paul was a witness at the time of the stoning of Stephen as they killed him. Stephen had the privilege of becoming the first Christian martyr for the Lord Jesus in the New Testament.

"And Stephen, full of faith and power, did great wonders and signs among the people." Acts 6:8, NKJV.

Persecution Began:

After they martyred Stephen in the presence of many people, a major fear took place in the hearts of all the Christian believers.

At that point, Paul was prepared to wipe out the entire Church of God. Going from home to home, he took out Christian followers of Jesus and forced them into jail.

Paul fought against the Christian Church in Jerusalem, and the Church experienced great persecution. This oppression, though, caused all the apostles and Christian believers to spread out throughout Judea and Samaria.

Paul finally traveled around to try to force the Christians and disciples in Jerusalem to be imprisoned.

Paul Met Jesus:

Eventually, he received letters from the Jewish spiritual rulers to send him to the Jews in Damascus. Paul was traveling there, and as he drew near to Damascus, a flash of light from heaven suddenly shone around him.

"Then he fell to the ground, and heard a voice saying to him, "Saul, Saul, why are you persecuting Me?" And he said, "Who are You, Lord?" Then the Lord said, "I am Jesus, whom you are persecuting. It is hard for you to kick against the goads." Acts 9:4-5, NKJV.

Because the glory of the Lord Jesus had shone down on Paul, it had blinded him. For three days, he lost his eyesight, and his colleagues had to show him the way into Damascus by hand. Later, Jesus directed Paul to go into Damascus.

Paul Arrived in Damascus:

When Paul, along with his colleagues, arrived in Damascus. The Lord told a believer by the name of Ananias to find Paul, lay his hands on his eyes, and restore his sight.

When Ananias prayed for him, immediately, Paul received his sight back, and he could see again.

"And Ananias went his way and entered the house; and laying his hands on him he said, "Brother Saul, the Lord Jesus, who appeared to you on the road as you came, has sent me that you may receive your sight and be filled with the Holy Spirit." Acts 9:17, NKJV.

God called Paul into a great ministry. He should go through many challenges in life so that he would preach the word of salvation.

Paul, with a Passionate Zeal:

The Lord had a special assignment for Paul to become a worldwide witness of Christ. After he had an excellent visitation with Jesus, his life turned into a dynamic experience with the love of God.

Paul got baptized, and he became a servant of the Lord and an apostle to the Gentiles. At the same time that the Lord called the apostle Peter to the Jews to preach the salvation of God.

Paul had a remarkable strength and a passionate zeal to preach the Gospel of Christ. He wanted to win the lost souls and all Gentile non-believers.

All Apostles welcomed Paul:

It is his messages that represent much of the New Testament of the Bible. Paul traveled to Jerusalem, where he met Peter, James, and John.

They knew of Paul's amazing transformation into a new life in the Lord. Now they would trust him and accept him into the assembly of the apostles.

Later, Paul worked with Barnabas to preach in the church in Antioch. The life of Paul was full of challenges and suffering for the sake of the Gospel.

On his early evangelistic trip, his finest achievement was planting many churches in Asia and the neighboring countries.

Paul Suffered Persecution:

Paul had God's favor in every area of his life, and God was with him. In Rome, they imprisoned him, and then they set him free. Later, he had an opening evangelistic meeting.

Paul came back to Rome, where he was arrested again and locked up for a couple of months alongside the apostle Peter in jail.

Paul endured persecution. By a request of Emperor Nero, Paul was executed with a sword.

Paul's letters were written to various churches throughout the area. He wrote thirteen of them, becoming books that now exist in the New Testament.

Many scholars have researched who was the original writer of the book of Hebrews. We don't know exactly who was the author of the book? But many believe it to be the apostle Paul.

The Book of Romans

THE MAIN THEME OF the book of Romans is God's plan of salvation. The righteousness of God carries justification by faith for all humanity. The essential truth of the Gospel to Jew and then to Gentile.

Although the evidence of justification by faith has been established. It could be considered that there was a greater message of the book.

Paul taught that salvation alone is the beginning of the Christian faith. He presented how to separate Christian believers from sin and death.

A plan of God was created and made available by the acceptance of Jesus. Receiving the forgiveness of our sins and living with Christ with no guilt and no condemnation. By allowing the presence of God and the empowerment of the Holy Spirit to dwell in our lives.

Relationship and Salvation:

Paul presented the primary structure of salvation to the congregation. He continued to point out the relationship between Jew and Gentile in God's design of redemption.

Christian Jews were being refused by the wider Gentile gathering in the congregation. Because the Jewish believers still were bound to follow the rules and religious ceremony.

Paul appeared to review the spiritual convictions of the Christian life. He reached the realization that Jews and Gentiles alike were sinners. They need the salvation that only comes from Jesus.

God arranged that salvation through Jesus and through His sacrificial act on the cross. The plan of God must be accepted by faith, which God has given to all mankind. Amen.

The Books of Corinthians

THE LETTERS TO THE Corinthians were pastoral letters that describe doctrinal and functional church issues. Jesus desires to be the center of the Church.

The congregation must be built on the Rock that is Christ. The Holy Spirit lives in the center of the Church, which is the body of Christ.

Paul wrote these letters to emphasize the discipline of the Christian and the fulfillment of holy communion. In the second letter, he described the New Covenant while he was staying in Ephesus.

Paul emphasized the death of Jesus on the cross and how He became alive again. Paul sought to encourage some groups of Christians who were trying not to attack each other.

Christians should care for other saints, and these necessary studies need to be taught in church meetings.

Caring for Each Other:

Paul described the character of pure love; it is consistently desirable for people to carry out their lives in love.

The Holy Spirit moves among Christians and builds up their faith so that they can achieve a better victory in their experience with God.

Paul's views and reactions as a church leader inspire Christians to have a fully unique approach toward these matters. He encouraged them to get rid of any images of false gods.

So, Christians must escape these factors perfectly. God has the ultimate offer to bring in a fresh love of life to their souls, the finished triumph over death.

The Book of Galatians

GALATIAN'S LETTER WAS WRITTEN because of a doctrinal situation occurring in the Church.

The congregations of that region needed a deeper understanding of the fundamental truthfulness of justification by faith alone. In which the Judaizers were rejecting it.

These legalistic Jews demanded that Christians protect the Mosaic Law. Specifically, the Judaizers insisted on circumcision as an obligation for Gentiles who wanted to be saved.

React to the False Teaching:

In many aspects, it was like they were saying you must convert to Judaism first, and then you would be acceptable to convert to the Christian faith.

When Paul heard that this untruth was being promoted in the Galatian churches. He wrote this letter to show our freedom in Christ. He reacted to the false teaching that the Judaizers were trying to use to draw people onto an improper path.

The Word has made it clear for us that we are justified by grace through faith. We have true power, and we have spiritual freedom in Christ.

We are not under the slavery of sin or the influence of the Old Testament Law. Paul condemned anyone who would criticize the grace of God or try to reform the Gospel.

The Book of Ephesians

THIS IS AN INTRODUCTION that would share with the part of the Christian discipline in this letter. It relates to our character in Christ.

Usually, those who are allowing themselves to be taught from this book receive more significant direction. It would lead us to spiritual growth and victory in the Lord.

This book emphasizes the spiritual warfare and the daily battle of the Christian believer.

As disciples of Christ, we must entirely recognize who we are in Christ. We must likewise prepare ourselves in the power of God's ability to preach the Good News to all humanity.

A Practical Way of Faith:

In Ephesians, Paul explains the study of the nature of God called theology. It should be a practical means to learn God's will for us and to live in a practical way of faith in Christ.

We must put our faith into practice, and we should understand who we are in Christ. We must live with the One True God who always existed, and we recognize Him, having a relationship with Him by faith.

Learning about the Book of Ephesians points out the relationship between accurate doctrine and good practice in the Christian life. Many people forget "theology" and instead wish to study aspects of "practical" life.

The Book of Philippians

THE MAIN THEME OF the Book of Philippians is joy. The messages of joy and rejoicing in the Lord always are presented in this book of the Bible.

We experience it and characterize the joy of the Lord as a fresh relationship between a Christian believer and the living God.

A study of the Book of Philippians encourages us to have a passion and thirst for Christ. Christians should be united in the spirit of humility, in contentment, and the joy of the Lord.

Paul strengthens us in Christ, and we should strive to be brought together. To have a closeness to one another in the same manner, helping and serving each other in the Lord.

Paul admonished us to have the same love, becoming like a servant, being one in spirit and purpose, united together.

Rejoice Always:

Let's turn away pride and greed but in humility. We must have aspirations higher than ourselves, seeking to serve and cherish one another.

Today, by Paul's teaching, if we accept his advice, it will not divide us into all our denominations. As Spirit-filled Christian believers, we experience the peace of God by casting all our cares on Him, and we continuously rejoice in His presence.

No matter what we are fighting or what difficult situations we face in our daily living. We must follow the Word of God, as it tells us to rejoice in the darkest hours of our lives. He can deliver us from our troubles.

The Book of
Colossians

THE THEME OF COLOSSIANS is the sovereignty and the supreme power of Jesus. The Church was under attack from wrong teachers who were dishonoring the divinity of Jesus.

They were teaching people that He was not really God. Paul was directed by the Lord to address these problems. The character and nature of Jesus Christ were that of the Creator, and Jesus is the Redeemer.

Paul explained with them and established his theory concerning this complex and challenging situation. It was important to him that this congregation experience God in His glory and majesty.

He wanted their spiritual eyes to be opened to the wrong teachers who were in their midst.

Salvation Completed by Jesus:

Paul's letter to the Colossians was written to educate Christian followers. He encouraged them that salvation is entirely and only found in Jesus.

The character of Jesus must be recognized precisely. He also wrote to remind them of all the acts of salvation has completed by Jesus.

It could only have been accomplished through His divine nature, which existed in the physical form of Jesus.

Jesus is the image of the invisible God, and no one experiences the unseen God unless He reveals Himself to that person. Jesus gave His life for all. As He died on the cross, and Christian believers can have faith in the completed work of Jesus.

Be Grateful in Christ:

Paul was teaching about the new and unique way of life in Christ that takes place through our divine union with Jesus. We are living the new life, changing from glory to glory, as we are receiving a new character as well as eternal life in Christ.

Paul reminds us to worship Him and be thankful for everything. As we recognize that He has forgiven us, we have peace with God.

Colossians presents Jesus as the Creator, the Mighty One. Paul lists His spiritual attributes and demonstrates that He is the head of the congregation.

We discovered the way of life in the Lord Jesus because He is the Bread of Life. Making the wrong decision outside of Christ leads to death. There is no new life that can be found without Christ. He is the true Word and Life.

The Books of Thessalonians

It describes the theme of two books of Thessalonians as *"the resurrection and the rapture of the Church."* This book describes Jesus to have predicted His return to His Church as taking place for Him at any hour.

He instructs us to be ready, standing by for the *"blessed promise"* that we will see Him one day returning in the clouds.

The Word speaks about the Day of the Lord, which indicates the end of time will be completed. This is the day when Christ will come back to the earth with all His saints.

We know that the word **'rapture'** is not mentioned in the Bible. But the meaning of the rapture is that we will be **'caught up'** with Him.

When we see Him in the air, but the meaning of His Second Coming is when we all, as saints of God, will come back to the earth with Him.

Strengthening one Another:

The primary theme of the book is **"strengthening one another."** Although the letters to the Thessalonians are recognized as the "Rapture books." In specific reference to their discussion of the return of the Lord to the earth.

Because the Thessalonian congregation was small. They had to go through some worry from both worldly rules and their relatives in the Jewish synagogue.

It might have occurred that, even though they were new in their faith in the Lord, they might struggle to continue their confidence.

The congregation must encourage one another and support each member of their group to keep working together and to put their trust in Jesus.

Praising God for their Faith:

The letters provide encouraging words to the congregation in the area of Thessalonica. Paul made the statement they should praise God for their faith in Christ. Hope in the Lord, and care for each other, and how they have grown into the life of Jesus.

Paul mentioned their sacrificial striving for the Gospel. His support for the Thessalonians whom he wished to visit again.

He expressed how they were acknowledging God in their faith, comforting those suffering oppressions in their present life. They should be praising God for their service and growth in the Lord.

Needed Devoted Themselves:

The congregation that had been established with a few Jews has transformed, but many came from old pagan worship practices.

Paul knew the church in Thessalonica was very young and that it needed much work on their spiritual teachings. He continued to carry out his work as a tentmaker and serving this church.

Paul related himself to be a minister who would feed this church with a word of encouragement.

He devoted himself, his soul, and his heart to the Thessalonians. They needed to believe that they would dedicate themselves likewise with a whole heart to God.

Paul expressed his happiness and confidence upon receiving a praise report of their excellent lifestyle. He urged them on in their expansion in the Gospel.

The Books of Timothy

THE THEME OF THE two letters to Timothy concerns accurate teaching and godliness with Christian character. False teachers had tried to split up the earlier congregation. Timothy was convincing them to handle this problem in a better way.

Paul encouraged Timothy to support a correct understanding of the Law and the Gospel of the Lord Jesus. Paul wrote in several forms of expressing how to carry out in godly activities.

He further invited Timothy to be involved in preparing his congregation to perform their service in a godly way. He stepped up to devote himself to explain an excellent with sound doctrine to his people.

This detail reveals the call for the minister's experience and how Paul had directed Timothy to handle the issue.

Living in Godliness:

In these letters, Paul calls for the setting up of godliness and purity for new leaders of the congregation.

He recommended to these new ministers that the way of life they lived would be perhaps the finest witness. It would cause the words they presented to have significance to other people.

The strongest quality a pastor can have is to serve others. Paul's emphasis here is that if a man has a dishonest spirit in his secret life. It will affect him and cause him to dishonor God in public.

If he lives with sincerity, not hiding anything in a quiet place, it performs a grace and will bring glory to God. Purity is a lifestyle that is established in the heart of ministry and continuing it will lead to holiness.

Paul said in his letter to Timothy to follow him as a model, that is to look at how he himself was serving and ministering.

Young Servant Must be Dedicated:

Paul mentioned that these new ministers should devote themselves fully to the truth.

Because by giving themselves wholly over to the demonstration of the Word, they would grow into the life of service.

The new transformation of his character would prepare us to be like Christ better. Paul spoke to the young ministers to continue preaching the Gospel and to cover themselves by the truth of the Word of God.

Paul elected the ministers of the Gospel, and Timothy was effective in looking after the flock and causing them to commit themselves to others.

Avoid False Teachings:

He knew that the truth of God must move forward, and that life becomes hardships. Paul encouraged Timothy to be steadfast and reliable.

As a minister to resist the temptation and with solid confidence and fought the good fight of faith.

Paul instructed them to continue teaching the Word with sound doctrine. They must recognize the false teaching that was taking place in the church at that time.

Paul was calling for Timothy to preach the Word. He was being equipped to protect the Church of God.

To teach the Word with the correct guidelines, and to preach the Good News to lost souls.

The Book of Titus

THE THEME OF TITUS is setting the church at Crete in place. Paul was mentoring Titus and building up a good leader, teaching him to make corrections and to establish order.

The congregations were experiencing a lack of leadership on the island of Crete. Paul was not trying to travel over there, but he was trusting Titus to organize everything and get things in order.

Titus was faithful as Paul's colleague in ministry, and he was also a Gentile, just as Timothy was.

Titus was young in the Lord, and Paul was guiding him in the faith. He was converted to Christ by Paul's ministry.

Assign Good Elders:

Paul was focusing on how to assign elders who had the qualities of an overseer. Paul expected these church members to be true *leaders, noble, sensible, honest, mature, responsible, and trustworthy.*

Paul instructed Titus to educate these people to be knowledgeable, and believers who would like to participate should do their part.

It's thoughtful to have members of all ages should have a passion for serving. Christians were to live wisely, and they should always be ready to worship God.

Paul was trying to challenge the believers to do a marvelous act of salvation. Paul insisted that they concentrate on godly living. We must go on doing what is good in response to God's grace to us in salvation.

Being Trustworthy Leader:

As Titus encouraged, we should have a magnificent love for every man of the Church who would be ready to serve.

We can learn how to minister to others because God has transformed us and given us a new life in Christ.

Paul knew he could depend on Titus; he was a trustworthy man. By God's plan, Paul was trying to plant churches on the island of Crete.

He was trusting God and looking to Titus as a leader. He was especially reliable in managing the Church, giving it a form of godly order.

Strong in Challenges of the Ministry:

Titus was standing strong in many challenges of the ministry. He was in a position in which he could learn more through Paul's early letters sent to him.

He gained strength from the Lord as he looked to be dealing with diverse cultural demands. Especially the people of Crete who were lived good lifestyles.

The book is small teaching that sets up a new plan in the local congregations of Crete, but even now, it allows us to have a statement about Christian living.

The Book of Philemon

THE THEME OF PHILEMON is forgiveness. We serve the God of forgiveness. Philemon describes Christ as our Lord and Master, who accepts us with His mercy and grace.

We do not belong to ourselves, to our own lives, but we belong to His eternal Kingdom. Paul wrote to Philemon with a brief message from Rome to remind him about the virtue of forgiveness.

Philemon had attended Paul's meeting in the city, and when he heard Paul's preaching, he gave his life to the Lord.

Philemon had a slave who was working for him, and at the same time, he had a desire to offer his home for the fellowship of the Church.

Philemon tries to Forgive:

Paul was giving Philemon some advice from the Lord about how to solve the problem of slavery. As we know, Paul was locked up at the time of the writing of this letter.

Paul had traveled to Ephesus during his ministry. Onesimus was a slave under the authority of Philemon; he had robbed his master, and then he ran away.

He had planned to go to Rome to meet Paul. Paul was encouraging him to go back to his master. Onesimus was still under the ownership of Philemon, and Paul felt that God had a plan for his life.

He witnessed to Onesimus, and he became a Christian. Paul urged Philemon to let go of all his unforgiveness and accept Onesimus as a brother in Christ, not as a slave.

Unify Brothers together:

Paul had instructed them that they had a duty toward their servants. He offered to unify both Philemon and Onesimus as brothers in Christ. With Christian respect so that salvation would become significant to them.

The Lord Jesus had provided the covenant of grace for everyone who would have faith. It would show obedience to God's Word and fellowship all together in worship. It's needed to have experience with a complete justification in Christ.

The Book of Hebrews

THE THEME OF HEBREWS is the complete superiority, sufficiency, and sovereignty of Jesus Christ. The Son of God was the advocate of God's grace.

He died on the cross and was raised from the dead. Jesus ensured our salvation, our redemption, our restoration, and everlasting life for every Christian.

He is our true Chosen One, and He draws us before the throne of God. He is sinless, and Jesus serves as our Mediator between man and the Father.

Jesus Shed His Blood:

Only Jesus sacrificed His blood for our sins. He accomplished and finished the work of salvation on the cross.

The Good News is that all the laws, traditions, and animal sacrifices in the Old Testament ended with the sacrifice of Jesus.

When we invite Jesus, the Son of God, into our hearts as our Savior. He forgives our sins, and cleanse, purifies us from all our unrighteousness.

It might be the starting point in our Christian walk. But we will have challenges, confusion, temptation, fear, and trouble in this world.

When we confess our faith in the victory. When we believe in Jesus for guidance, He is ready to strengthen us in the time of difficulties. We can grow strong in faith and build up with a fruitful spiritual life.

Be Truthful and Faithful:

Faith is gratifying to God, and when we declare our belief, the grace of God will be abundant.

"Now, faith is the substance of things hoped for, the evidence of things not seen." Hebrews 11:1, NKJV.

God has fulfilled His promise to give His Son as a sacrifice for Salvation. He calls us to endure despite temptations, to survive through trials. When we have the struggles of life, spiritual battles, and He encourages us always to remain faithful to Him.

We can experience that God is always truthful, faithful, and that He has made up a glorious home for us.

The Son as an Heir:

God created the entire world through His Son, Jesus. God chose the Son as an heir. Jesus is the perfect reflection of God's character, and He is the Light of God's glory.

Jesus saves all men by His mighty Word, and He has made purification for our sins. He has received a powerful name that is above all names.

He is now seated at the right hand of the Father. He is ready to perform as our Great High Priest; He is superior over all kings. His reign and His realm of duty are in the divine temple.

His sacrifice on the cross cannot be repeated. He is the gift of life, and His sacrifice was perfectly acceptable to God.

Everlasting Life:

The everlasting redemption that Jesus has purchased for us by His own blood. The same love He had in the Old Covenant, this doctrine is covered under the grace in which Christian believers rejoice to live.

Jesus would give them the promise and the power to enter the kingdom of everlasting life.

The Book of James

THE THEME OF JAMES is faith 'set in action,' it must be practical, honest, and pure. Justification is fully completed with a sincere belief, which comes naturally in true works.

Let's look at what James is saying to be able to identify just before the eyes of men. James made a significant point in describing the challenging experience that the works of the law can justify no man.

Paul was expressing the idea of man's performance in proclaiming one's righteousness in the sight of God.

Faith without Works is Dead:

We recognize as we read the Book of James that a test is given to true believers of Jesus. It is not just "talking to walking," but it is saying that we must act in our faith to work out our own salvation.

Being truthful in our faith walk means growing in the spiritual authority of the Word. James encourages us to concentrate on the phenomena of the Word of faith, how it works in our life.

He excites us to carry out the Word of truth. He testifies that faith without works is dead, and that good works are not the source of our salvation.

"For as the body without the spirit is dead, so faith without works is dead also." James 2:26, NKJV.

"Born-again" Experience:

Salvation has been given to us through an act of the grace of God. In which we are washed and cleansed by the blood of the Lamb of God. We confess our sins to the Lord Jesus; we invite Him into our hearts.

Then the Holy Spirit comes to dwell in our lives. When after these things take place, God forgives our sins and gives us a new spirit.

This is called a **"born-again"** experience in the Lord. True faith in God will usually bring confidence in our hearts and our spirit. It is not just a philosophical theory; it is a significant factor.

James explains the basic nature of the relationship between faith and works. He wrote that he placed the complex truth that the works of the law can justify no one.

The Books of Peter

THE BASIC THEME OF the books written by Peter is experiencing victory in life, even during suffering and oppression. Peter wrote that we should seek confidence as he pointed out the gift of our glorious salvation in Jesus.

Peter encouraged the followers who had been broken up throughout the ancient province. They were under extreme oppression for the sake of believing in the Lord Jesus.

Peter recognized the persecution; he himself had been broken, intimidated, imprisoned, and locked up for preaching the Word of God.

Keeping Good Confidence:

Peter had learned to be faithful in the Word, to remain strong, and move forward without bitterness. Without giving up his loyal faith, keeping good confidence, and living with a triumphant life.

The power of enduring faith is in the word of Jesus, who is the One who teaches us to secure a great victory in Christ. It provides the promise of everlasting life to all Christian believers.

One way to relate to Christ is to experience His suffering and to share His word of love to the world.

Stand Strong in Present Time:

Peter revealed that His way was truly a life of rejoicing, even though this season of oppression had been terrible. He reacted when he saw an opportunity for delight in God.

When we go through hardship for the sake of Christ. We can remember what our Savior went through for us.

We see this message established as the evidence of Peter's special encounters with Jesus and his exhortations. He explained the devil as the major attacker of every Christian believer in the present time.

The promise of Jesus' future coming provides us with encouragement and hope. This is the remarkable way of the grace of the Lord related to us. He endured the pain, agony for us on the cross.

We stand up to believe that Jesus is truth, and we exalt the name of Jesus when the world and Satan try to harm us.

"Be sober, be vigilant; because your adversary the devil walks about like a roaring lion, seeking whom he may devour." 1 Peter 5:8, NKJV.

Victory Come out of Suffering:

Peter had suffered through a crisis, and he was saying that in the time of difficulty, the Lord would empower us to get closer to God.

He would manifest His protection, and His mighty glory would come out of Christian persecution and trouble.

We get more encounters with the Lord Jesus when we are persecuted. Our relationship with the Holy Spirit grows stronger. Peter learned the relationship between oppression, comfort, and celebration in victory.

In all our difficulties and tribulation, we can recognize that God is accomplishing His perfect plan for us. He is making spiritual warriors out of us. God allowed His own Son to go through suffering on the cross.

He wants us to have His grace and eternal life. His grace is a new life filled with joy and peace in the Holy Spirit. Amen.

The Books of John

THE THEME OF THE three books of John is
that God is love. He is the root of love. Love is
the nature of His presence and being. John was
pointing out that for our rejoicing, we shall op-
erate in the love of God.

We would have no desire to sin, that we
would be aware of wrong teaching. We would
recognize that we have eternal life by accepting the Son of God as our Savior in the name of
Jesus.

We know that John had an extremely convincing word about this tremendous revelation
of life in the name of Jesus. He says that Jesus
has stepped into human life and touched our
souls.

Covered us By His Blood:

John wished that all of us would run into the
life of Jesus. As Jesus walks in the light, we will
also walk in the light of His glory with Him. The

spirit of darkness shall not stand against the Light of God.

When darkness decides to come toward us, we can declare that the blood of the Lamb of God covers us. His blood has protected us from the attack of the enemy.

Then we will walk with Him in victory, and we will receive a fresh anointing of His Spirit and be transformed by Him.

Solid Relationship with Jesus:

The apostle John had a powerful fellowship and a solid relationship with Jesus. As we know Him, the Lord is instructing us with His true Word and His love toward us.

We all can have that vital connection with Jesus. John presents these letters from his statements. Which were based on the evidence of the actual truth and understanding of the Lord?

What would appear to be true of the Word affects our times because the Word is the truth? John speaks the truth of His Word to us, causing us to live with joy and peace in Him.

He describes to us how Jesus entered this world as the Son of God to establish harmony with God and men. Therefore, through His grace, His forgiveness, and His passion. He will love us again, and He will adopt us as a child of God.

He Watches over Us:

If we choose the words of God as John wrote them. Suppose we commit ourselves every day to the true love of the Lord. He promises to have fellowship with us and comfort us.

John further realized that that involved revealing our sins and pursuing God's mercy. We must depend on God to restore our lives from sin, along with accepting our mistakes against others and making our faith right.

Another powerful part of spiritual growth is to experience God in a personal way. So many people feel that Jesus is far away from them and that He is in a long-distance relationship with them.

Some people have tried hard to find Jesus in prayer and in reading His Word. But we remember the Lord is near to us. We always need to recognize that He cares for us.

I believe that He looks after our worries and our daily struggles, and He watches our crises. He is the One who solves all our troubles. Amen.

The Book of Jude

THE STUDY OF THE Book of Jude is false teachers and leading the congregation through a time of extreme apostasy. The Book of Jude is an extraordinary piece of writing for us today because it was actually recorded for the end-time church.

In fact, it started the church of the Lord on the Day of Pentecost. Jude recommends that we continue following the faith. It will be found that many false prophets are in the church.

Jude is short but significant writing filled with true knowledge, and it was recorded for the Christians of today. Jude's purpose was to convince them of the false teachers who had penetrated the Christian people.

He suggested inviting Christians to continue being solid in the faith and engaging in the truth of the Lord. Jude had a great experience with Jesus' salvation, and he was eager to write about His goodness.

Strong in the End Times:

This statement found in the Book of Jude stands for the finished work of Jesus for all Christian believers. Christ described His teaching, afterward moving on to the apostles.

Jude's statements were to warn the Body of Christ of an approaching, growing, and potential risk of false teachers.

He urged us to overcome our spiritual warfare. We need to realize that we should acknowledge the spiritual warfare that exists. To stay strong through these days of the end times.

We continue to have an extraordinary letter from Jude that can serve us as we face the unspeakable challenges of getting along in the end times.

Continue Moving Forward:

We Christians must cover ourselves from false teachings that can so easily deceive us. We all have a desire to experience the Word and the Good News of the Gospel, and we need it to keep us safe and guard us.

We receive the Lordship of Jesus in all aspects of our lives. It signifies the way we live to make us a transformation through Him. By our true faith, we always express His presence.

Our life in Jesus should reach our character as we lay down our own desires at the feet of Jesus, the Savior, and our Father.

We desire that intimate relationship with Him alone; we will have His blessings. We will continue moving forward to receive more victory. In Jesus' name. Amen.

The Book of Revelation

THE THEME OF THE Book of Revelation, also called the Apocalypse, is the ultimate finished destruction of the world.

It generally refers to the revelation of the apostle John, who also wrote the Gospel of John and three other letters in the New Testament. John's passion developed into a leader in the early Church.

He had apparently recorded his documents after most of the separate New Testament records were already written. It certainly indicates that the revelation was given as a message in a global letter.

The leading information in most of the message is a document in which John told of his dreams. There is no other book that can be described as the Book of Revelation.

John given Vision on Patmos:

Patmos is found geographically on a small Greek island in the Aegean Sea. The important site of the vision given to John and the place where the Book of Revelation was written.

The Roman Empire had dominated Asia Minor, and Patmos was in a province on the western border of the region of Turkey. There had been several breaks in the persecution of the Roman rulers.

God would entirely wipe out the evil persecutors of His Church, especially the Roman Empire.

Introduction:

Revelation 1:1-20, John says that his writing is a revelation handed over to him by Jesus through an angel.

John moves into a rapturous excitement, and he encounters the vision of the Lord Jesus that he indicates in the Book of Revelation. He receives a vision of seven golden lampstands.

John received a vision for the future to come. It has given as inspiration for the suffering

Christian Church so that they would have the promise of God for protection.

Seven Prominent Places:

The Book of Revelation is extraordinary and unique in the whole Bible. John wrote the Book of Revelation to be handed out among the Christian congregations in seven prominent places in Asia Minor: **Sardis, Laodicea, Ephesus, Smyrna, Pergamum, Thyatira, and Philadelphia.**

This book contains full knowledge of God. Its purpose was to inform and explain the plan of God to the world. Including what would happen in the millennium.

Reassuring Christians Believers:

Revelation provides encouragement and confidence to Christians that God is fully in authority. When the time is perfect, He will totally wipe out the forces of evil that work to influence our world. God's everlasting kingdom will take its full and final place.

In essence, John's vision presented reassurance and happiness to the oppressed Christians of Asia Minor. He encouraged them that their difficulty was not meaningless.

God would surely triumph and crush the Roman Empire that had led to their exploitation.

The Gospels contain Jesus' instructions, and other letters tell of His teachings. But in Revelation, Jesus, Himself appears to talk straight to the congregations.

The Seven Reports:

The Son of God speaks seven words for John to deliver to the seven congregations in Asia Minor. It presents several changes to each of the seven congregations.

Each message praises the faith community for its strengths and encourages public members to work on their vulnerabilities.

"To the angel of the church of Ephesus write, 'These things says He who holds the seven stars in His right hand, who walks in the midst of the seven golden lampstands." Revelation 2:1, NKJV.

A Throne in Heaven:

John received a dream of an open gate to heaven. He looked at the throne of God with its everlasting praises. He received a scroll with seven seals in the right hand of God.

But there was no one found trustworthy enough to open it except the Lamb. The Lamb opened the seven seals of the scroll. As the Lamb opens each seal, it tells one condition of individual misery and an individual future.

The Seven Seals:

White Horse: This is the appearance of Jesus as He starts the first of the seven seals, holding a scroll filled with God's judgment. The first horseman was sitting on a white horse and bearing a bow. He obtained a crown, and He overcame.

"And I looked, and behold, a white horse. He who sat on it had a bow; and a crown was given to him, and he went out conquering and to conquer." Revelation 6:2, NKJV.

Red Horse: This horseman was given the power to remove peace, and people would annihilate each other with the sword.

"Another horse, fiery red, went out. And it was granted to the one who sat on it to take peace from the earth, and that people should kill one another; and there was given to him a great sword." Revelation 6:4, NKJV.

Black Horse: The balance scales indicated a tremendous rise, but the oil and wine were spared.

"When He opened the third seal, I heard the third living creature say, "Come and see." So I looked, and behold, a black horse, and he who sat on it had a pair of scales in his hand." Revelation 6:5, NKJV.

Pale Horse: Death has the spirits of the dead with him. One-fourth of the earth would be slain by the sword, by drought, and by the wild beasts and creatures.

"So I looked, and behold, a pale horse. And the name of him who sat on it was Death, and Hades followed with him. And power was given

to them over a fourth of the earth, to kill with sword, with hunger, with death, and by the beasts of the earth." Revelation 6:8, NKJV.

Martyrs Cry Out: The martyrs cried out, how long? Not yet, not until the numbers of fellow servants, their brothers, and sisters, to be executed were completed.

"When He opened the fifth seal, I saw under the altar the souls of those who had been slain for the word of God and for the testimony which they held. And they cried with a loud voice, saying, "How long, O Lord, holy and true, until You judge and avenge our blood on those who dwell on the earth?" Revelation 6:9-10, NKJV.

Heavenly Signs: Earthquakes take place, the sun darkens, the moon changes into red, and stars fall from the sky.

"I looked when He opened the sixth seal, and behold, there was a great earthquake; and the sun became black as sackcloth of hair, and the moon became like blood." Revelation 6:12, NKJV.

Rapture: Heaven will be silent for about half an hour.

"When He opened the seventh seal, there was silence in heaven for about half an hour." Revelation 8:1, NKJV.

"And they heard a loud voice from heaven saying to them, "Come up here." And they ascended to heaven in a cloud, and their enemies saw them." Revelation 11:12, NKJV.

144,000 Faithful Men Sealed by an Angel:

It is believed that 144,000 will reach out to preach the eternal Gospel over all the earth. They will preach the message of salvation and judgment.

The glory and fear of God are being carried upon the earth. These people who get saved are the believers in the Lamb of God. It will restore them from among the people without guilt.

"And I heard the number of those who were sealed. *One hundred and forty-four thousand* of all the tribes of the children of Israel were sealed." Revelation 7:4, NKJV.

The Lamb and the 144,000:

"Then I looked, and behold, a Lamb standing on Mount Zion, and with Him one hundred and forty-four thousand, having His Father's name written on their foreheads." Revelation 14:1, NKJV.

The Seven Trumpets:

- **The first angel sounded:** And hail and fire followed, mingled with blood, and they were thrown to the earth. And a third of the trees were burned up, and all green grass was burned up. Revelation 8:7, NKJV.

- **Then the second angel sounded**: And something like a great mountain burning with fire was thrown into the sea, and a third of the sea became blood. Revelation 8:8, NKJV.

- **Then the third angel sounded**: And a great star fell from heaven, burning like a torch, and it fell on a third of the rivers and on the springs of water. Revelation 8:10, NKJV.

- **Then the fourth angel sounded:** And a third of the sun was struck, a third of the moon, and a third of the stars, so that a third of them were darkened. A third of the day did not shine, and likewise the night. Revelation 8:12, NKJV.
- **Then the fifth angel sounded:** And I saw a star fallen from heaven to the earth. To him was given the key to the bottomless pit. Revelation 9:1, NKJV.
- **Then the sixth angel sounded:** And I heard a voice from the four horns of the golden altar which is before God. Revelation 9:13, NKJV.
- **Then the seventh angel sounded:** And there were loud voices in heaven, saying, "The kingdoms of this world have become the kingdoms of our Lord and of His Christ, and He shall reign forever and ever! Revelation 11:15, NKJV.

The Woman and the Dragon:

"So the great dragon was cast out, that serpent of old, called the Devil and Satan, who deceives the

whole world; he was cast to the earth, and his angels were cast out with him." Revelation 12:9, NKJV.

The Beast out of the Sea:

"Then I stood on the sand of the sea. And I saw a beast rising up out of the sea, having seven heads and ten horns, and on his horns ten crowns, and on his heads a blasphemous name." Revelation 13:1, NKJV.

The Beast out of the Earth:

"Then I saw another beast coming up out of the earth, and he had two horns like a lamb and spoke like a dragon." Revelation 13:11, NKJV.

"Here is wisdom. Let him who has understanding calculate the number of the beast, for it is the number of a man: His number is 666." Revelation 13:18, NKJV.

The Three Angels:

The first angel said: saying with a loud voice, "Fear God and give glory to Him, for the hour of His judgment has come; and worship Him who made heaven and earth, the sea and springs of water." Revelation 14:7, NKJV.

And another angel followed, saying, "Babylon is fallen, is fallen, that great city, because she has made all nations drink of the wine of the wrath of her fornication." Revelation 14:8, NKJV.

Then a third angel followed them, saying with a loud voice, "If anyone worships the beast and his image, and receives his mark on his forehead or on his hand." Revelation 14:9, NKJV.

Harvesting the Earth:

"Then I looked, and behold, a white cloud, and on the cloud sat One like the Son of Man, having on His head a golden crown, and in His hand a sharp sickle." Revelation 14:14, NKJV.

"And another angel came out from the altar, who had power over fire, and he cried with a loud cry to him who had the sharp sickle, saying, "Thrust in your sharp sickle and gather the clusters of the vine of the earth, for her grapes are fully ripe." Revelation 14:18, NKJV.

Seven Bowls: *God's Wrath*

First bowl: "So the first went and poured out his bowl upon the earth, and a foul and loathsome sore came upon the men who had the mark of the beast and those who worshiped his image." Revelation 16:2, NKJV.

Second bowl: "Then the second angel poured out his bowl on the sea, and it became blood as of a dead man; and every living creature in the sea died." Revelation 16:3, NKJV.

Third bowl: "Then the third angel poured out his bowl on the rivers and springs of water, and they became blood." Revelation 16:4, NKJV.

Fourth bowl: "Then the fourth angel poured out his bowl on the sun, and power was given to him to scorch men with fire." Revelation 16:8, NKJV.

Sixth bowl: "Then the sixth angel poured out his bowl on the great river Euphrates, and its water was dried up, so that the way of the kings from the east might be prepared." Revelation 16:12, NKJV.

Seventh bowl: "Then the seventh angel poured out his bowl into the air, and a loud voice came out of the temple of heaven, from the throne, saying, "It is done!" Revelation 16:17, NKJV.

Babylon, the Whore on the Beast:

"Then one of the seven angels who had the seven bowls came and talked with me, saying to me, "Come, I will show you the judgment of the great harlot who sits on many waters" Revelation 17:1, NKJV.

"And the woman whom you saw is that great city which reigns over the kings of the earth." Revelation 17:18, NKJV.

Grief over Fallen Babylon:

An angel declares that the fall of Babylon is approaching and urges the loved ones to escape the place to flee the destruction. Those who have taken an interest in their contact with Babylon regret her leaving.

"And he cried mightily with a loud voice, saying, Babylon the great is fallen, is fallen, and has become a dwelling place of demons, a prison for every foul spirit, and a cage for every unclean and hated bird!" Revelation 18:2, NKJV.

Hallelujah over Babylon's Fall:

A great multitude in heaven was rejoicing with a song of honor. They praise God for the

falling of Babylon, who declared His righteousness and judgment.

**"After these things I heard a loud voice
of a great multitude in heaven, saying,
"Alleluia! Salvation and glory and honor and
power belong to the Lord our God!"** Revelation
19:1, NKJV.

**The Rider on the White Horse Defeats the
Beast:**

John looks on as the heavens are opened, and
a rider on a white horse emerges. The rider is
called *"Faithful and True."*

**"And He has on His robe and on His thigh a
name written: KING OF KINGS AND LORD OF
LORDS."** Revelation 19:16, NKJV.

**"Then the beast was captured, and with
him the false prophet who worked signs in
his presence, by which he deceived those who
received the mark of the beast and those who
worshiped his image. These two were cast alive
into the lake of fire burning with brimstone."**
Revelation 19:20, NKJV.

Satan Is Bound for a Thousand Years:

John looks on as an angel captures Satan and throws him down into the dark abyss. Satan is completely detained for a thousand years so that he will no longer lead people away from the faith and their life with God.

"Then I saw an angel coming down from heaven, having the key to the bottomless pit and a great chain in his hand. He laid hold of the dragon, that serpent of old, who is the Devil and Satan, and bound him for a thousand years." Revelation 20:1-2, NKJV.

After a Thousand Years:

Satan is freed and released to deceive the nations of the earth for a short time. Again, Satan is forced into the fire with the other two beasts to suffer day and night forever and ever.

"The devil, who deceived them, was cast into the lake of fire and brimstone where the beast and the false prophet are. And they will be tormented day and night forever and ever." Revelation 20:10, NKJV.

The Judgment of the Dead:

John saw all the dead rise before the white throne. They were all judged according to their life and their works, as indicated in the Book of Life.

"And I saw the dead, small and great, standing before God, and books were opened. And another book was opened, which is the Book of Life. And the dead were judged according to their works, by the things which were written in the books." Revelation 20:12, NKJV.

"And anyone not found written in the Book of Life was cast into the lake of fire." Revelation 20:15, NKJV.

A New Heaven and a New Earth:

John looked at the new heaven and a new earth, and a new Jerusalem came down from heaven. God would settle among the people.

"Now I saw a new heaven and a new earth, for the first heaven and the first earth had passed away. Also there was no more sea. Then I, John, saw the holy city, New Jerusalem, coming down out of heaven from God, prepared as a bride

adorned for her husband." Revelation 21:1-2, NKJV.

The New Jerusalem and the Lamb:

It describes the new holy city in all its richness because God and Christ shall be there. Therefore, all saints of God will worship the Almighty God in His presence.

"And he carried me away in the Spirit to a great and high mountain, and showed me the great city, the holy Jerusalem, descending out of heaven from God." Revelation 21:10, NKJV.

"I Am Coming Soon":

Jesus said to John, **"And behold, I am coming quickly, and My reward is with Me, to give to every one according to his work. I am the Alpha and the Omega, the Beginning and the End, the First and the Last."** Revelation 22:12-13, NKJV.

Conclusion

I CONCLUDE THIS BOOK with the great honor of being able to write many encouraging stories. I believe these compelling stories to lead us to a high level of achievement by the leadership of the Lord Jesus.

This book shows how to receive more spiritual insight from the main characters in the Bible's stories. The leadership of the Holy Spirit has recorded every word.

I have tried to summarize each book with a short review from the Word of God. Each record in the Bible can inspire us to know the Lord Jesus better.

As I wrote this book, the Spirit of God has been present ever since I started until now. I believe it will be a blessing to all of you. The anointing of the Lord is living inside this book.

I am convinced, with a humble heart, that this book will bless you. Many of you who are trying to read this book will receive a greater anointing of knowledge, and it will revive your spirit.

The Word of God is a living Word, and He will speak to you in a personal way. He is making you a magnificent inspiration of His glory from these stories.

This book will encourage, inspire, and prepare you to become a mighty man or woman of God. Sharing powerful stories about the men and women of God from the Bible can teach us how we can stand strong in this present life.

May the contents of this book serve you and help you grow in the confidence of your faith in Christ. This book will reach millions of Christian believers around the world. Thank you.

About the Author

DR. DANIEL KAZEMIAN HAS dedicated his life to the nonprofit organization International Evangelistic Ministry, to preach the Good News by the anointing of the Holy Spirit. In June 1993, he was ordained to the ministry in the National Church of God by Dr. T. L. Lowery in Washington, DC.

He has since become one of today's most dynamic charismatic preachers. Christ walked into his life in January 1985, and Daniel was transformed into an exciting, enthusiastic dynamo for God. He's passionate about sharing God's love and saving grace with everyone, as well as healing the sick.

Daniel started his evangelistic career and his radio/TV ministry in Denmark-Scandinavia and abroad. He is now serving in the prophetic and healing ministry, and he ministers in churches, seminars, conventions, crusades, and anywhere the Spirit of God leads him.

Daniel earned his associate degree from the National Bible College and Seminary in June 1993 in Fort Washington, Maryland, and a bachelor's degree, a master's degree, and a Doctor of Theology degree from the International Theological Seminary in July 1996 in Plymouth, Florida.

He is the president of the nonprofit organization, International Evangelistic Ministry, located in Gainesville, Georgia.

Contact him through email:
ieministry@hotmail.com

Visit our website:
www.InternationalEvangelisticMinistry.com

www.ingramcontent.com/pod-product-compliance
Lightning Source LLC
Chambersburg PA
CBHW051940090426
42741CB00008B/1217